A Voice For Veronica

Jeanette Woods

A Voice For Veronica
The story of Veronica Knight,
the first victim in the Truro murders
in South Australia

This story is dedicated to the Forgotten Australians

A Voice For Veronica: The story of Veronica Knight, the first victim in the Truro murders in South Australia
ISBN 978 1 76041 705 5
Copyright © Jeanette Woods 2019
Cover painting © Peter Woods 2018

First published 2019 by
Ginninderra Press
PO Box 3461 Port Adelaide 5015
www.ginninderrapress.com.au

Contents

Acknowledgements		9
Foreword		11
1	1976: A Train	15
2	1974: An Introduction	18
3	1975: A Parting	28
4	1972: A Meeting	32
5	1976: A Shopping Trip	36
6	1977: Missing	41
7	1977: An Accident	49
8	1978: A Discovery	52
9	1978: A Funeral	57
10	1979: A Search	60
11	2018: A Mounted Police Officer	68
12	1979: An Arrest	72
13	The 1970s: Forgotten	78
14	1980: A Verdict	90
15	1980: An Editorial	100
16	2017: A Plan	103
17	October 2017: A Reply	106
18	2017: A Connection	110
19	2017: A Trip	112
20	2017: A Grave	121
21	1974: A Parolee	125
22	2017: An Officer	129
23	2017: A Matron	134
24	2008: A Death	139
25	2017: Forgiveness	142
26	2017: Dorothy	147

27	2017: A Pilgrimage	153
	Appendix	159
	A discussion of some questions arising from this story	159
	References	174
	Bibliography	176
	Thanks	178

Speak out on behalf of the voiceless, and for the rights of all who are vulnerable.

Proverbs 31:8

We are called to speak for the weak, for the voiceless.

Martin Luther King Jr.

If you want to tell untold stories, if you want to give voice to the voiceless, you've got to find a language.

Salman Rushdie

The darker the night, the brighter the stars, the deeper the grief, the closer is God!

Fyodor Dostoyevsky

Acknowledgements

Many people have contributed to the writing of this story. A number of them, in fact, became part of the story as it unfolded and have generously permitted me to include them in the evolving narrative. Thank you especially to Brian and Ruth for their memories of the happy times we shared with Veronica and the important role they played in her life. I am grateful to Ken Thorsen for his assistance with many aspects of the case from a police perspective. I am indebted to Charles Cornwall for his generous encouragement and expert information on the parole system. Nicola not only helped me find the most important person in this story, but her warmth and professional care blessed us on the way to Truro. She also led me to Harry, the mounted police officer, who willingly shared his personal story with me. Thank you to Viktor Bohdan for allowing me to use his wonderful courtroom sketches that were featured in the newspaper at the time. My heartfelt thanks go to Dorothy, who was willing to revisit a painful past to help me to explore and come to terms with it.

Then there are my first readers, Carolyn, Naomi, Ruth and Peter, as well as the good friends who have believed in this project – Lorraine, Amanda, Rosemary and many others.

My family has been part of my journey, humouring my unexpected exploration of a confronting event. Most of all, I am so grateful to my ever-supportive husband, Peter, who also became part of the story himself and joined me in researching this project. His special contribution as the visual artist in the family is the wonderful portrait of Veronica on the cover.

Although I take responsibility for this book, it truly was a team effort.

I also wish to acknowledge all those who played a part in Veronica's life and cared for her in various ways. We may not have met, but this book is for you as well.

Foreword

Veronica was my young friend. I knew her for less than three years but she has been in my heart ever since. From time to time, I leaf through her photograph album and wonder how a life can leave so little behind. More than forty years since her body was found in the quiet Truro bush, I am left still wondering why I have not explored her story before now.

My desire is that, having been forgotten for so long, she will be remembered in a small way by my writing this book. With scant information to work with and the barriers of privacy legislation working against me, I wondered if I would have enough material to write a story. I just knew that I had to start. I discovered, however, that her story is just one of the many stories about persons who go missing and eventually are recognised as victims of crime. I had no idea where this exploration would ultimately take me.

It was never my intent to rake over the horrors of what are now known as the infamous Truro murders, although reading everything I could find was part of the journey I undertook in order to write this account. To read about the awful detail of the evil perpetrated on Veronica and six other young women was painful, to say the least, and yet a necessary part of my research. I was, however, determined to focus on Veronica, rather than on the details of Australia's worst serial murders.

There are books and TV series about the actions of two men who have both now died. There is only one account by a family member of one of the girls: I acknowledge the book by Anne-Marie Mykyta, *It's a Long Road to Truro* (1981). Her account of the agonising loss of her daughter, Julie, and the long wait for closure, moved and inspired me to persevere in my writing for Veronica.

Photographs in the media at the time show the other parents leaving court after the conviction of James Miller on six counts of murder. I did not know, however, if anyone was there for Veronica. Because Christopher Worrell, the killer, died in a car accident in 1977 (thus bringing the killings to an abrupt halt) he was never charged with his crimes. His accomplice, James Miller, was charged with all seven murders as part of a 'joint criminal enterprise' but was not convicted for Veronica's murder on the grounds that he could not have known with certainty that it would happen. As a result, no one has ever been made legally responsible for her death.

My hope is that Veronica's short life will be remembered, not for a shockingly notorious series of events, but for her youth and enthusiasm, her faith and the special place she had in our family. Everyone who knew her remembers her bubbly nature and zest for life. As I recently published my long autobiography, I feel deeply the contrast of her truncated life with my own story. I would like to be remembered and understood by later generations and have had more than seven decades to make my mark in the world. I was able to pursue my education and had a successful career; I leave a large family of children and grandchildren whom I love and by whom I am loved. All that was taken from Veronica, whose life and line came to a sudden, premature and tragic full stop. We will never know what she could have accomplished in a longer lifetime, and she has left no progeny to keep her memory alive.

So this story, set as it is against the heartbreaking backdrop of the summer of 1976–1977, aims to give a voice to Veronica. This book turned into a profound journey for my husband and me when we travelled to Adelaide for the purposes of research, expecting to clarify my memories and perhaps to trigger some long faded recollections. Amazingly, I managed to meet up with some key figures in the story, and it was wonderful to discover how much she was loved.

That week was a series of serendipitous – even miraculous – opening doors of discovery, and I was to find that the circle of victims is very wide – it includes us. I know that the act of forgiveness is a key to being free from the sadness. It had taken forty years for us to connect properly with our need to do just that; it was only then that we were able to undertake the pilgrimage to the Truro bush and make our peace.

Jeanette Woods
August 2018

Miss Veronica Knight.
Sutherland Lodge Hostel.
341 Angans St. Adelaide.
SW 5000. 19-12-1976.

Dear Jeanette a Peter a Naomi.
I hope you are well and keeping fit.
Thank you for the lovely letter.
I ~~will~~ will be coming on the train
I will leave here on Sunday night
and arrive on Monday the date is
26-12-1976 — and arrive on the 27-12-1976.
in the morning.
Looking forward to seeking you.
Lost and lost of love from.
Veronica Knight.

xxxxx x xxxxxx
xxxx xxx
xxx
xx

1

1976: A Train

'I'm going anyway,' said Peter. He could not accept that there was no point in meeting the train.

I was not surprised that he wanted to go and made no attempt to stop him – I also wanted to remain hopeful and could not contemplate the worrying alternative.

The Overland from Adelaide rolled into Melbourne's Spencer Street Station, as Southern Cross Station used to be called. A comfortable overnight ride before air travel became a cheaper option, the train was a popular route between the cities, arriving conveniently at breakfast time at platform 1. On this Monday morning, 27 December 1976, Peter scanned the snaking carriages as they decelerated past him, looking at the windows for a glimpse of the lanky teenager he was hoping to meet. When the train finally came to a stop, passengers spilled out onto the platform, heaving their suitcases and heading for the exit, breathing deeply in the morning air after an air-conditioned night of rocking on the rails. He walked back and forth, looking anxiously and waiting impatiently until the very last person had disembarked and the platform had emptied once again. It was ominously quiet.

He walked the platform again, and then with sinking heart found a payphone and called me. 'She didn't come,' he said.

Veronica was not there and, with that realisation, our fading hopes were dashed. We knew that she had booked her ticket weeks before Christmas and had been counting the days, hours and minutes until this train trip to Melbourne and her holiday with us; we knew with certainty that she would not have missed the train for any reason in her control.

The phone call that we received the day before from Brian and Ruth, our friends in Adelaide, had shocked us. They told us that Veronica had mysteriously disappeared and would probably not be on the train to Melbourne. She had not arrived home at her hostel, and was last seen shopping in the evening the day before. We still hoped that she would somehow be on that overnight train, that we would meet her, and that all would be well. Trying to think of rational explanations that were not sinister, we had hoped that there was a reason that we could not imagine and that Peter would go to the station and find her – it would all become clear. Imagine how disappointed she would be if she were on the train and no one was there to meet her.

We needed to find and look after the eighteen-year-old whom we had left behind in Adelaide the previous February. I was over seven months pregnant when we left Adelaide, with our first baby expected to arrive a few weeks later in April. Veronica was so sad when we departed for Melbourne and had been saving money and counting the days all year until she could spend time with us and our beautiful baby.

After all, Veronica saw Naomi as her little sister. Her disappearance just made no sense to us – it was inconceivable that she would change her mind about coming, especially without letting anyone know.

Peter came home from the city and was very quiet. We sat down and hugged each other.

'What do we do now?' he asked as we cuddled Naomi and held her a bit more tightly. Veronica had desperately wanted to have time to play with this little girl.

'We could phone Ruth again to see if there's any more news,' I suggested. I felt sure that they would have heard something by now and the mystery would be solved. But then, wouldn't Ruth and Brian call us immediately if they had anything to tell us? The questions went round and round in my head and I tried to think of scenarios that might explain the inexplicable.

'Maybe something came up from her family that was really important?' I said hesitantly, because I knew that it would not have happened. 'Perhaps a girlfriend took her to stay at her place and she lost track of time?' I didn't think that idea was at all likely. 'She could be terribly sick and not have been able to tell anyone,' was my next improbable suggestion.

Peter then said that although it was unlikely, she could have met someone, even a friend, and been offered a lift to travel here, and was still on her way. We almost took for granted the fact that we might not have heard anything because communication was often difficult.

We just had to try to be patient and believe that our young friend would suddenly reappear, grinning as she usually did, and that everything would be fine. We were running out of ideas and the happiness of our Christmas celebrations the day before with our family faded as we felt increasingly puzzled and concerned. Sixteen months of silence would follow before we would know why she wasn't on that train.

2

1974: An Introduction

The church in Beulah Road, Norwood, an inner suburb of Adelaide, was our second home in the early years of our marriage. We were young, keen, unencumbered by children, and loved nothing better than spending time with the young people at St Bartholomew's Anglican Church.

Peter and I met in 1971 at the Adelaide Bible Institute in Victor Harbor and, for me, there had never been anyone else. We fell in love, were engaged and married within a couple of years. We decided to establish our home in beautiful Adelaide, even though our respective families were in Sydney and Melbourne. As newly weds, we began to forge our independent life together, establish our marriage, grow vegetables and make a home.

In its heyday, the huge and picturesque stone church next door to our rented home in Beulah Road had housed a large congregation and a Sunday school of over a hundred children. As was the case with many inner suburban churches, attendance had declined and the landscape of the suburb had changed and Norwood, conveniently located a few minutes from the city, had become rather gentrified and semi-industrialised. There were not as many children in the church now and we saw that as a challenge. Our response was to start a new gathering for the kids, called Bart's Club, aiming to make it a fun time with lots of activity as well as teaching and interaction. We hoped it would thrive and grow. As well as the children's program, we began to meet informally with a few young people after church for music, chatting and supper.

'How are we going to attract new young people into our group?' I

wondered as we relaxed with our mugs of Milo after a full Sunday of busy activities. We had finished the day with our rowdy youth meeting in the old rectory next to the church.

Very soon after that, Ted, the rector, had some news for us. 'The Allambi Hostel around the corner has contacted us to say that there's a young person who has just moved in and wants to attend our church. Would you like to make contact with her?'

'I'd love to,' I replied immediately. 'Give me her details and we'll follow her up.' This was just what we wanted. What I did not realise then was how significant this chance encounter would be.

We had to find some time to visit Allambi in Osmond Terrace, but that was not easy with us both working full time with different work rhythms. I was teaching at a Lutheran secondary school, mostly English and some drama. I studied at Melbourne University in the 1960s, graduating with a BA, Dip. Ed., and taught for three years in the Victorian country town of Heywood before heading off to Victor Harbor to train for cross-cultural work. After the three years of study there, I had completed a postgraduate BD and the college diploma.

Peter was a residential care worker, involved in the care and social well-being of teenage delinquents who were incarcerated in a government institution called McNally Training Centre. While at college, we had both joined a team that visited the institution in a voluntary capacity and that had helped to fuel our desire to work with disadvantaged youth. Once Peter had a job there, he worked in shifts, so our daily cycles were often at odds, adding to our time pressures.

I phoned the hostel and made a time for us to visit Veronica after work. We pulled up outside and looked at the building. Like much

of Adelaide architecture, Allambi hostel was built in earlier times – a double-storey mansion with pillars and verandas, partially covered with ivy. Norwood was an old suburb and many of the wide, tree-lined streets with grassy median strips had graceful, large buildings on each side. The hostel was used from 1947 as a boarding home for girls who were wards of the state and who worked in the city. Allambi is an Aboriginal word meaning 'a quiet resting place' and it was meant to be a secure place for the girls to transition to their adult working lives. After a few years in the 50s when it was used for girls from Vaughan House reformatory, it returned to the former purpose from 1961, this time for school-age girls.

The girls were looked after by a matron but had a degree of freedom in being able to go out and to pursue outside activities. As in earlier days, there was an expectation that the residents would attend church as part of their accountability, perhaps in the hope of forming positive relationships and a supportive community. So when we were asked to go to meet her, it was probably part of her orientation in the hostel.

'We've come to meet Veronica Knight,' Peter said to the matron, who met us in the entrance hall.

The building was austerely decorated inside, with a shadowy feel in the foyer that made me hope there was more light filtering into the other rooms. We sat in the heavily padded chairs and waited for Veronica to appear. I had no idea what she might look like, nor even if she genuinely wanted to meet us.

'Hi,' she said as she loped down the stairs. She was taller than I expected and rather gangly with her long legs. Thin features and straight dark hair framed her freckled face and dark eyes, and she dressed like a typical teenager. Her grin split her face, giving her a cheeky look we came to love. She seemed excited.

'Why don't you sit in the lounge?' suggested the matron, and beckoned us through the arched hallway.

I was glad to see that the lounge was sunnier and felt like a comfortable meeting place; I was thankful that the girls had some pleasant spaces in the hostel, and hoped it was more like a home than some of their previous experiences might have been.

Veronica was fidgeting and perhaps a little nervous to meet strangers.

'I hear you'd like to try out our church,' I tried as an opener. 'We're just around the corner – maybe you've seen the big building in Beulah Road?'

There was no response for a moment.

'Is there any other girls there?' she asked. The slightly inaccurate grammar and her awkward, diffident manner gave away her lack of education. I suspected that she would struggle with literacy and that her school experiences had been patchy at best.

'A few, and we're looking for more so that we can have extra activities,' said Peter.

She thought that sounded good, and I explained to her the events she might be interested in. After some chatting, we offered to come and pick her up the following Sunday and agreed on a time. I didn't ask her anything about her background, or where she had stayed before she came to Allambi. It was hard to know whether she would feel sensitive about questions like that, so we just decided to let things take their course for the time being.

On the way home, we talked about the teenager and wondered whether she would be ready when I called on Sunday morning, and, more importantly, whether she would enjoy her first outing with us.

'Do you think she really will come?' I asked Peter as we got dressed to leave for church; we had to hurry to allow time to pick up Veronica on our way.

'I reckon she'll be waiting on the steps – she was excited to meet us and have something to look forward to,' was Peter's response.

We drove around the corner the next Sunday, and, sure enough, she was there, peering out at the gate and happy to see us when we arrived. We parked in front of the imposing church building and introduced her to a few people, and she came in and sat close to us. Some of the older folk disapproved of us calling our group Bart's Club, perhaps feeling it was somehow disrespectful to tradition and the saint. Moreover, the music was all accompanied by Peter's guitar and my accordion; when we later brought the kids into the main church service to sing to the congregation, there was a murmur of concern about instruments other than the historic organ being played in church.

To use up some surplus energy and simply to have fun, we started each meeting with some games – the more physical the better. Poison ball, brandy and relays were popular and when we were all played out, we would move on to some singing and teaching, then finish with some group work and often craft activities.

Our feeling about Veronica was that, although she was sixteen, she would enjoy being part of Bart's Club. Clearly, her level of education was low, but her social development was also behind her age and in many ways she was like a primary school child. Over time, however, we realised that any delay in her developmental growth was due to lack of opportunity and that she was perceptive and quick to understand many things. So we took her out with us to Bart's Club in the hope that she might develop into a young assistant for the smaller children. And that's just what happened.

Veronica quickly won our hearts and began to be a part of our lives. She would phone me several times during the week and then obtained permission to stay with us over weekends. Sometimes that was a mixed blessing – we loved her, but she chattered incessantly and wanted to relate to us when I sometimes needed space to recover from my teaching week. Her favourite activity was to bake with me and we made all sorts of delicious cookies and cakes, which she loved to take back to the hostel. She was happy to hang out at our place, accompany us to the shops and share drives in the car together; she just wanted to be with us. We began to be the family she didn't have.

Bart's Club was the highlight of her week. The children were accepting and she just fitted right in – competitive when they played games, interested in the teaching presentations and especially keen on the craft activities. She was clearly accustomed to helping younger children and loved nothing better than assisting the little ones who came. She surprised us at times with flashes of insight and little bits of wisdom – she had been fending for herself for quite a while.

One day Peter raised the issue of our need for finances for the kids' club. 'What can we do that involves the kids and will raise some money for all the things we need to do? How about a lamington drive?' he said nonchalantly to me one day, as if we could miraculously create lamingtons with unskilled labour and make a profit.

I had a funny feeling that I was about to develop some new skills as a caterer. 'I love those kids, but they would make a huge mess and I would have to work out all the recipes to make good lamingtons,' I responded, knowing that we would probably go ahead and do it.

Veronica insisted that she would help us, but I wasn't sure that her assistance would make it any easier – organisation and details were not her strengths.

We launched the drive and collected an astonishing number of orders from church members, family and friends – then we had to figure out how we would pull off the creation of hundreds of lamingtons from scratch.

After some research, I decided that the best way was to order big slabs of pre-baked sponge cake so that we could estimate accurately how many of them we would need. Then I would experiment with chocolate icing and somehow make a perfect batch that was enough for coating all the emerging lamingtons, and ensure that we had enough coconut for the final rolling.

Veronica was excited and jumping around by the time the day arrived to make the lamingtons. The children arrived and we set to work with several long tables and an assembly line. Disposable gloves had not been invented back then, and I think we just tried to insist on clean hands. What followed was a hectic few hours of chaos and fun with a great deal of chocolate and coconut everywhere, but the result was the huge total of orders being filled and delivered by the end of the day. Veronica was in her element and declared it the best day of her life.

Soon after that we planned a camp: we would organise it, run it and cater for it ourselves. Veronica was desperate to come to the camp and managed to gain permission to be part of it. She wanted to help me with the cooking, and I was grateful for any assistance – Veronica loved to be needed. The camp was a great success, although the place we stayed in was rather damp and basic. Veronica and I produced some great food in the simple kitchen, and she loved all the activities we had prepared for the kids, like tie-dyeing T-shirts. It was, after all, the 70s.

She especially loved the times when we made music. Along with the accordion and guitar, we also had a large collection of percussion instruments, and it was probably the first time Veronica had experienced playing in a band of sorts. She even stepped in one day to save a little

girl from a bad fall – she was used to watching out for others and the now grown-up child and her parents still remember the incident with gratitude. Veronica made a beautiful card for us after the camp, to thank us for allowing her to go with us.

> To Dear
> Mrs and Mr Woods
> Thank you for
> The lovey camp
> and good spech
> Love from Veronica
> knight ♥ XXXX.

So it was that our relationship with her developed as we became good friends and grew to be something between mentors and informal foster carers for Veronica. Allambi was still her home base but she lived for the times she could be with us and we knew the emotional attachment was strengthening for us all. She was looking for a loving social environment, something she had lacked in her short life, and we were happy to provide just that.

She often needed a lift to events or to return home and we helped as we could but were also aware that she had to conquer public transport and to be confident in looking after herself. There was always a small concern that in spite of her bright personality and ability to talk her way through any situation, she was also a little vulnerable in her childlike desire to please and to be friendly. We warned her against talking to people she didn't know and tried to educate her to be healthily vigilant on buses and the streets. She, however, would brush off our concerns – just as any teenager does to her parents – and laugh at our cautions.

'Veronica just asked me how somebody gets confirmed,' said Peter one morning.

'I doubt that she has any idea what it means. She's just heard us talking about it.'

'Well, she wants to join the church and says she wants to do it with you.'

From then, we prepared together for the big day. My confirmation was to make me a member of the Anglican Church, which was necessary for me to be in a teaching role – so for me, it was a formality. Veronica, however, went shopping to find a new white dress – an option for those who wanted to wear something special – and we made plans to go to St Peter's Cathedral in the city together on Sunday afternoon 1 December 1974. There was a large crowd for the special occasion and we had some friends from St Bart's who sat together with Peter to support Veronica, me and four others from the church who were presented for confirmation that day. I remember standing in the aisle with my young friend – she nervously held my hand tightly as we inched forward towards the front of the beautiful cathedral. We were such an unlikely pair as we professed our faith together that Sunday in the city of churches.

3

1975: A Parting

Towards the end of 1974, we had to move from our rented house next to the church across town to Everard Park, which was closer to my work, but further from Norwood and all our connections. Veronica managed to catch public transport to see us – we were right on the Glenelg tramline – and still stayed with us as often as she could. As we shared more of our lives together with Veronica and our relationship with this loveable and energetic teenager grew, a little cloud began to form. When Peter and I met, we both had a strong sense of 'calling' to work overseas in other cultures and that desire had not diminished. The only question that had puzzled us since our marriage was to which part of the world we would go.

Not wanting to be tied down in Australian suburbia and its attendant trappings, we had made choices that kept us free from many of the obligations that burden a young married couple who are just setting up a home. Community was the buzzword, and for a while, we had shared our home with another needy young person who was looking for somewhere to stay. We had also sourced cheap or free furniture for our rented home that we could easily give away and, in due course, we were accepted to work in Irian Jaya in Indonesia with the Church Missionary Society and were planning to train for that work in Melbourne. From there we would go to Java for language study and, finally, to Irian Jaya to work.

So we knew that we would be leaving Adelaide in February 1976 and that Veronica would not be able to go with us. It simply would not be fair to her, nor in her best interests, to allow her to become emotionally dependent on us – and that was beginning to happen. We knew that she loved us and that we had helped her to grow in many ways, but we did not want to repeat what might have happened to her over and over since she was tiny – she would form an attachment and then lose it when she was moved to yet another foster home or institution. How could we wean her from us without causing her more pain?

Almost more heart-rending for her and us was the fact that I was pregnant. After nearly two years of marriage, we were ready to think about a family, but quite daunted when my ability to conceive was called into doubt. Defying all odds, I was pregnant within weeks, and our baby was due in April 1976. Veronica was so excited, and considered the baby to be almost like her younger sibling. She watched my tummy begin to swell and was filled with anticipation, planning all sorts of gifts for this special babe.

It just seemed impossible to explain to her that we would be leaving and that the baby would not be born before we left Adelaide. Nevertheless, we owed it to her to prepare her for the parting, and the best we could do was to promise her that she could come and visit us in Melbourne and enjoy a short time with us and the new baby.

We discussed our concerns with Brian and Ruth, our new pastor and his wife who had arrived in 1975 with their family of four children, and asked them whether they felt they could draw Veronica into their family life when we left, and if we could start the process of a gentle handover right away. We had to make it as easy as possible for Veronica, but knew that we would have to be intentional about the process. I felt sure that Ruth would be a wonderful substitute mum for our girl.

They agreed and we began to arrange for Veronica to be with them and their children a little more often, and to start lessening our contact. It wasn't easy, as she could not really understand why she couldn't do baking as often at our place and stay with us every weekend, or why we didn't always pick her up for events, but we persevered for her sake. After many conversations and explanations, Veronica began to understand our plan a little more.

She knew that Brian and Ruth had lived and worked in Tanzania,

Brian and Ruth.

and now understood that we were going to Indonesia. Her geographical knowledge was scant, so she, in her endearing way, fused the two together and used to talk about us going to 'Tanzanesia'. She had little information about either place, so we tried to teach her about our destination, but realised that with minimal formal education it was very hard for her to accumulate facts in a meaningful way.

'If I can't go to Tanzanesia, then I can go to Melbourne and see you before you go,' she would say. 'Are you going to Melbourne first? When are you leaving? How far is it? Which month will the baby be born? Can I come over as soon as it's born? What are you going to call it? Little Veronica?. Where would I stay in Melbourne?' and so on, over and over as she tried to make sense of what lay ahead.

She found it hard to stay quiet for very long but when she stopped peppering us with questions, I knew that in her rare moments of silence, she was thinking about it all. Both she and we knew that we were about to be separated by distance and culture.

Meanwhile, Ruth promised to keep an eye on her, to help her to write letters to us and to make arrangements for Veronica to come and see us after the baby was born. At least Allambi was just around the corner from the rectory and Veronica would be able to walk around to see her. I knew that Ruth and her family would be good friends for her, and would feel as protective of Veronica as we were.

I finished teaching at the end of the year and we began to pack up our house in preparation for our departure to Melbourne and then overseas. We would be leaving all our lovely Adelaide friends behind and knew we would miss them, but leaving Veronica was going to be the hardest wrench for us as well as for her. With only weeks to go before the arrival of our baby, we finished our packing, said our farewells and hit the road for Melbourne, the first stop on our long journey to Indonesia. The promise to Veronica was that we would see her at Christmas time and she began to count the days.

4

1972: A Meeting

On 2 February 1940, a child was born in the west end of Adelaide, the oldest of six. Melville (on his police record, but Melvyn in his own account) Raymond Just's early life did not go smoothly, and by the time he was eleven years old, he was in the Magill Reformatory for housebreaking, shop-breaking and multiple counts of larceny. At fifteen, he was stealing cars and motorbikes, charged on over ten occasions and continuing to steal, and while still not an adult, doing hard labour in Long Bay Prison, south of Sydney in NSW. He returned to Magill at sixteen. He ran away, he truanted, he broke and entered and stole, over and over again, finally graduating to Yatala, Adelaide's adult prison, by the time he was seventeen. The litany of offences on his police record continues through to 1975. Sadly, he was not alone in being shaped by the prison culture – of forty youth in Yatala when he arrived, he notes that ninety-five per cent had been in Magill with him.[1]

His childhood was harsh and his young friends got into as much trouble as he did, but his fast bowling in cricket earned him the nickname of 'Killer'. Sadly and ironically, James William Miller, as he was later known (he changed his name by deed poll in July 1976), was a product of the same government system that delivered him to be incarcerated, as was Veronica, who suffered from being institutionalised for all of her short life. The difference was that Veronica never broke the law.

On 7 January 1954, Christopher Robin Worrell was born. Miller later said that Worrell told him that his conception was the result of

Christopher Worrell.   *James Miller.*

his mother being raped and that consequently he had never known his biological father and was brought up by his grandmother. When he was six, his mother married again and the young boy was adopted into the new family unit, taking his stepfather's surname. They moved several times, as Mr Worrell was in the RAAF, but finally settled in Eden Hills in the bushy foothills south of Adelaide, where young Worrell attended Blackwood public schools.

He followed his father's career and joined the RAAF, but was discharged because he was 'incompatible with service life'. His discharge in Western Australia was followed by a string of casual jobs. In March 1974, he was placed on a good behaviour supervised bond and given a suspended sentence for the conviction of armed robbery of a twenty-year-old female hitchhiker.

His probation and parole officer, Mr Charles Cornwall, noted in conversation with me in 2017 that at the first interview in the Probation and Parole Office, Adelaide, when Worrell was twenty years old and on a good behaviour bond, he was baby-faced, neatly dressed, respectful and had many questions. He found him 'cooperative' and 'forthcoming' and anticipated that he would likely be compliant. 'How wrong I was!' was his comment in his book of memoirs as he reflected on the dramatic turn of events that was to unfold.[2] Cornwall visited his family as part of his supervision of Worrell, and described his stepfather as domineering and his mother as gentle and nice, but rather deferential to her husband.

Only a few weeks later, Worrell was back in court, charged with attempted rape and indecent assault. Mr Cornwall recalls the court sentencing by Justice Sangster, during which he referred to Worrell as 'a miserable and contemptible creature'.[3] The suspension of his two-year sentence was revoked and another four years added, making a total sentence of six years in Yatala Labour Prison. He applied once for parole and was denied, partly because his parents refused to take him back home. After a second application in October 1976, he was granted parole, after serving less than two and a half years of his six-year sentence.

When James Miller was imprisoned for two years in Adelaide Gaol in 1972 for shop-breaking, he met twenty-year-old Christopher Worrell for the first time, and they moved into the same cell and became 'blood brothers'. Worrell was in prison at that stage for the rape and armed robbery. This intersection of their lives spawned a perverse association that would culminate a few years later in terrible violence. Miller's new friend told him that he was a psychopathic killer, yet Miller pursued the relationship with the younger man. As the friendship developed, Worrell described his lonely childhood and how he would love to have known his real father. Miller was released first after a short sentence and tried to go straight, even finding himself a job. Miller was upset that Worrell had been given such a lengthy sentence, and, against the rules, visited him in Yatala Prison, where Worrell had been transferred, until his friend was paroled early in October 1976. When they were both released from prison, they worked together and eventually lived together in a strange and deviant codependency.

This meeting of the two men in 1972 and their subsequent relationship was to have catastrophic consequences. Paul Wilson, in his book *Murder in Tandem: When 2 People Kill*, opens the chapter on the Truro murders with this description of the two men:

There could be no clearer example of hedonistic killers than James Miller and Christopher Worrell. Fulfilling every criteria by Dr Edward Green (*The Intent to Kill: Making Sense of Murder*), Miller and Worrell took several lives for excitement or pleasure… They may or may not have considered themselves God-like in their domination and elimination of their young female victims, but certainly their actions were those of people with no morality, compassion or concept of responsibility to society. The characters of these men who committed the Truro murders, as they became known, also strongly fit the dominant/submissive personality pattern typical of tandem killers; in fact, their relationship became the lamest of excuses by the surviving partner for his involvement in the murders.[4]

This relationship started in prison and, for Miller, ended in his own death, still in prison. Worrell's death in a car accident brought his murderous activities to a halt, which prevented the number of killings from escalating further than it did. Miller always maintained that Worrell was a personable friend, but that a 'dark mood' would come over him and then he would become a different person. There were rumours of a brain clot and some sort of heart dysrhythmia sustained from a motorcycle accident, but no official record was ever presented, and I cannot see an obvious connection. Miller apparently bowed to the younger man, and was in the end judged to have been part of the 'joint criminal enterprise' carried out by the pair over the summer of 1976–77. These events would become known as the Truro Murders.

The police never believed that Miller was merely a bystander. He drove the car for Worrell and says that he went on walks while the crimes were committed. He knew, however, what his partner was capable of and, at the very least, facilitated the crimes. Most people find it hard to believe his assertions that he was not involved in the murders, in spite of his plea in the title of the book he wrote in prison, *Don't Call Me Killer*.[5] These two men were an example of a close friendship that became unhealthy and, ultimately, a platform for indescribable wrongdoing.

5

1976: A Shopping Trip

Veronica and her friend Jenny were excited about their shopping expedition into the city on the evening of 23 December 1976. Captain Reed, the matron of their Salvation Army hostel, followed them to the door, where they hung their keys on the way out, and reminded them of the need to take care – there would be crowds of people in the city that night in the pre-Christmas rush. She told them to look after their belongings and not to talk to people they did not know. Both girls were excited as they disembarked from the bus and joined the throngs in Rundle Mall. It had only recently been closed to traffic and made into a pleasant pedestrian area, and there were many new shops now. 'What are you looking for, Veronica?' asked Jenny.

'I need some new tops and shoes and a special dress to go to Melbourne. I can't wait to see Peter and Jeanette and baby Naomi – it's going to be fantastic. I miss them so much.'

Veronica thought about the paper folder containing the rail ticket she had bought over a week before, carefully placed in the drawer in her room at the hostel in Angas Street. Only three days to go before she would be on the train and speeding towards Melbourne. It would be the furthest she had ever been from home and her first time out of South Australia.

The girls shopped and wandered as girls do, looking longingly at the shop displays and buying hot snacks to eat as they strolled down the mall and into City Cross Arcade. Half the population seemed to be in the city on the night before Christmas Eve, as the weather was warm and the long sunlight hours of the summer solstice made for a pleasant evening. The pair were in no hurry to get home to the hostel, although they were well aware of the 11.30 p.m. curfew. When the shops finally closed, the girls headed for the bus terminals at the western end of the mall.

'We'd better get to the bus soon, or we'll catch it from Captain Reed,' Jenny said to Veronica.

They knew better than to run late getting home to the hostel, because the matron always stayed up until they were safely home. She was like a mother hen with all her chickens under her wings. At that moment, however, they became distracted when they spotted a black-and-white photo booth and decided to take some photos together – the nearest thing to selfies in those days. Veronica had cut her long dark hair and had a new, short and curly hairstyle, making her look suddenly older. They crowded into the booth, giggling, and put their shopping down while they snapped the four shots they could take for their coins in the slot. Veronica started with a serious look and then began to smile into the camera. Jenny leant into the photo behind her, smiled and then made a face, and then they waited for the printed photos to come out of the slot before leaving the arcade. She put the photo strip away in her handbag.

Realising that time was moving on, they dashed off towards the bus stop in King William Street, when Veronica pulled up suddenly, looked down at what she was carrying and said, 'My shopping! I left a bag in the photo booth.' She had left the special dress in its wrapping on the bench in the booth and she would not go home without it. Like any teenager, she wanted her new things to take on her Melbourne holiday.

'You go ahead, Jenny, and if I don't catch you, tell Captain Reed that I'm coming on the next bus.' She turned round and went back to the booth in City Cross Arcade to recover her package.

That was the last time Jenny saw her, as she never reached her home at Sutherland Lodge. According to her testimony in court, Miss

June Tait, a Minda nurse and close friend, received a phone call from Veronica at around 10.30 p.m., but we will never know what was said, and there is no other mention of that call. Miss Tait has passed away now.

We also know from James Miller's account that she went to catch the bus in front of the old Majestic Hotel at 100, King William Street, and met Worrell, who offered her a lift home. When Miller drove past, they got into the car and Veronica was never seen again. We do not know why she ignored all advice and accepted a ride, but she was possibly concerned about the time, and may have felt safe because she thought that the two men were a father and his handsome son, as Miller was nearly twice Worrell's age.

All she had with her was a small bag with $180 in her purse – a considerable amount equivalent to around $1,000 at today's value – which was her money for the trip. Her purse was never found, there was no sign of the package she went to recover and it was never retrieved.

Matron Reed was immediately worried when Jenny returned without Veronica. She was more concerned about Jenny's safety when they had gone out and the warnings were aimed at her, but Jenny was home safe and there was no sign of Veronica. Despite the late hour, the matron found a small address book in Veronica's room and began to phone her Adelaide friends to see if she had decided to stay the night. She didn't care that it was late – she just knew that she had to find Veronica. She really couldn't believe Veronica would not have let her know – she was a girl who kept the rules and had always been responsible. The matron remembers even now, forty years later, that Veronica kept her room immaculate and dressed nicely. It was only ten weeks since she had moved into the hostel, but she had won her way into the hearts of the community of working girls and students, who cared for each other.

Captain Reed felt more and more agitated and went to her assistant Loretta's room. She did not want to disturb her as they both worked hard and were up early every morning to cook the girls' breakfast, but she needed to make a decision. 'Veronica's not home. She went back to the shops to get a parcel and didn't come home on the bus. She's never been late before. Her key's still hanging on the board and I've rung all her friends. No one knows anything and I'm really worried,' she said to Loretta.

They discussed the situation as quietness settled over the hostel and the residents turned their lights off and went to sleep. Jenny couldn't tell her anything else. What would they do? She didn't know where to begin and could hardly start looking on the city streets at such a late hour. They did not want to unsettle the other girls without any definite news.

At 1 a.m., the matron finally went to the police and was told that no report would be filed before the first twenty-four hours had passed. Uneasy and too worried to sleep, she went to bed and prayed. She knew she would need all her energy for the next day and that Christmas celebrations and meals would keep her extremely busy. Nevertheless, she returned to the police station the next day on Christmas Eve, and filed a report. The matron did not intend to let the matter go, as she knew in her heart that something was very wrong.

The report of missing person says that the form was filled out at 9 p.m. on 24 December 1976. The form was filed into the system on Christmas Day – in those days, it just joined thousands of other such reports in a filing system.

She returned yet again on Christmas morning to press for action. She had services to attend and lunch to cook for the girls remaining in the hotel and no spare time, but she persisted. The police roster also was minimal for the holiday period. The shops in the city had all been closed since the night before, and there is no record of any investigations or questioning taking place. Our address in Melbourne was included in the report but, inexplicably, no one from the police ever contacted us. There were plenty of people on the street where Veronica was last seen, but we will never know if anyone saw anything. She was gone.

With a heavy heart, Captain Reed contacted Brian and Ruth at the church and told them the disturbing news. Like everyone else who knew Veronica, they were sure that something was amiss, because they had helped to plan her trip to see us. They phoned us in Melbourne on Boxing Day, 26 December, and told us the disturbing news. She would not be on the train that night.

From a surprising source, James Miller, comes a moment of reflection, albeit too late:

> How was I supposed to forget Veronica? I wondered who she had been. This particular girl had been, for me, just another one Chris had cottoned onto as he had on more occasions than I cared to count. I did not even know her second name. Did Chris...? Would people be looking for her, asking questions, after she had not returned to the boarding house? Had anyone seen her get into our car?[6]

Indeed. And yes, there were people asking questions from 11.30 p.m. that night onwards, including Matron, Brian, Ruth, Veronica's friend Jenny, and Peter and me, but it would be a long time before those questions were answered.

6

1977: Missing

Between 2008 and 2015, over 305,000 people were reported missing in Australia, an average of 38,125 per year. Youths aged between thirteen and seventeen were the most likely to be reported; half of all those reported missing in that time were in this age group. Ninety-eight per cent are ultimately located, and most are alive.

A missing person is defined as 'anyone who is reported missing to the police, whose whereabouts are unknown and there are serious concerns for their safety'.[7]

In a research brief written by Bruce Swanton et al. for the Australian Institute of Criminology in 1988, the concept of missing persons is explored. It is noted that, in the past, it was considered that twenty-four hours or more should be let pass before serious investigation was undertaken, in the belief that most young people will return home or be found in that time. More recently, those early hours after a person is noticed to be missing are thought to be critically important in finding the person. It was recommended that it be mandated that missing person reports accepted by police be actioned instantly.[8]

Another issue that needs further research is the classification of missing persons. A lost person may actually be a victim of crime, as in the case of Veronica, but there are no clear guidelines for when one becomes the other, except if the body is found and foul play is suspected. It is, of course, too late for the victim by that stage. The various states of Australia use differing categories for missing person statistics, and a further confounding issue is whether or not absconders from institutions are included in them. In South Australia, they have been added, meaning that the larger aggregated total number blurs the boundaries, and thus, possibly, the responses to missing person reports.

There are many factors which will determine how urgent the response to a missing person report should be; a short list would include 'disability', 'endangered', 'involuntary' and 'juvenile' as the top criteria that would indicate urgency.[9] Veronica ticked the first three, and, at eighteen, was just above being classified as a juvenile, although her developmental age was probably lower. Her disappearance was reported by a person responsible for her care and safety in the early hours after she disappeared the night before, and she had no history of running away. She was left alone in the city after separating from her friend, making her very vulnerable. There was clear evidence that she had plans for the next hours of her life that were extremely important to her.

Yet she was not found for nearly sixteen months after her disappearance. Captain Reed reported to the police immediately when Veronica had not come home. Her shopping friend, Jennifer Marie Porter, returned home on her own and told those concerned exactly where Veronica had been when they separated. She did not vanish mysteriously from an unknown place – she disappeared somewhere between a specific photo booth in City Cross Arcade off Rundle Mall and the bus stop on King William Street on her way home. The minister of the church she attended, Brian, knew her well and Veronica had even lived with his family for a month earlier that year in June. They and all the church members at St Bartholomew's in Norwood knew and loved the lively lass who had been part of the congregation for over a year.

There was plenty of evidence that Veronica was extremely unlikely to be a runaway – but there seemed to be minimal response to her disappearance and I have found no evidence of any questioning of the public or interviewing in the area where she was last seen. Later on, after the terrible killing spree was discovered and the seven missing girls were found to be part of a frightening pattern of violence, the media began to portray the young women as girls who were out of control, wandering around at night and making themselves vulnerable. This was patently not true, and we knew it, as did the grieving parents of each of the murdered girls.

For Veronica, there were no immediate family members to draw attention to the case – only friends and the matron. We ourselves were a long distance away in Melbourne, and later went overseas, having minimal contact in the days before emails and media technology. It is still a mystery to me that we did not follow up more, even from so far away.

Clearly, she was planning to catch the train to visit us, and the money she had spent on the ticket just a few days before was considerable for her budget. Yet perhaps even we had some little doubts and wondered whether she had been drawn away by friends who were not a good influence. In fact, we hoped that was the case, rather than the awful alternative that we could hardly bear to contemplate. For the police, the family is the immediate source of information and there are protocols for keeping them informed. The emotional pressure brought to bear by the parents of a missing girl must be part of the motivation for police officers to pursue every avenue. When the photos were published much later after the court case that convicted one of the murderers, my heart felt heavy to see shots of each set of parents leaving the courts – but none for Veronica.

When we look at the public interest in the high-profile case of the abduction and murder of Daniel Morcombe in Queensland in 2003, and the police resources applied to it, by comparison it is clear that Veronica's case attracted minimal response. Daniel was only thirteen, and seen as a vulnerable juvenile, and was also abducted waiting for a bus (as were most of the Truro victims). In his case, his parents, Bruce and Denise, went public early and often, and persevered until he was found, even though it took some time. A dummy dressed in similar clothes was set up where he was last seen, and over the course of the case, members of the public made 20,000 calls to the police. The government offered a reward of $250,000 and another $750,000 came from a private donor, ensuring that the case was kept in the public arena.

No parents spoke up for Veronica, and no reward was offered until the Mykyta family, the parents of another victim, decided to speak to the media in 1979, over two years after Veronica disappeared and a year after her body was found. One key difference between Veronica and Daniel Morcombe's cases was that DNA played a part in the identification of the murderer in the latter, and the breakthrough DNA technology only began to be used in about 1986. There were no physical forensic clues to lead police to either Miller or Worrell.

While a motive for the killings can only be guessed it is certain the lack of publicity about the first disappearance gave the killer the confidence to strike again and again. The police accept now that a public alert and publicity at the time of the first disappearance might have prevented the later ones. However, their saturation effort on the case now contrasts starkly with the apparently offhand and routine approach adopted at the time of the disappearances.

'With the advantage of hindsight I would like to feel more could have been done,' says Chief Superintendent K.L. Thorsen, the officer-in-charge of the investigation.

> When you take the disappearances in isolation, they stand right out from the others at the time but with the others they are impossible to see. The sheer volume of missing person reports alone – about 3,000 annually – makes it hard to see things like this.[10]

The disappearances continued for seven weeks after Veronica went missing.

Tania Ruth Kenny was a fifteen-year-old student who had just completed Year 10 at St Peter's Girls' College and was reported missing by her family on 2 January 1977. Tania left her home on 31 December for New Year celebrations on the south coast, although her parents were not happy about her plans. After a busy social time with friends, she was last seen boarding a bus in Moana to return to Adelaide. A bus driver remembers seeing a girl who looked like her boarding his bus, but there were no further sightings and she was never seen again. Her family did not want any publicity and there was no communication with the media about her disappearance.

Julie Mykyta was sixteen (although the media erroneously stated that she was fifteen) when she was last seen in King William Street in the city on 21 January. Her parents, Irush and Anne-Marie, had encouraged her independence and adventurous spirit. On that day, she had been selling jewellery in the city with a friend and decided to stay in the city with another friend. She phoned her parents at about 9.30 p.m. to let them know and they asked her to be home by 11 p.m. She headed for the bus stop around 10.30 p.m., intending to catch the bus home in good time. Her friend saw her talking to someone in a white car, then get into the car and be driven away. She was never seen again. Her parents tried in vain to draw attention to her disappearance, but it was treated as a typical runaway teen incident, especially when it emerged that she was in the habit of hitchhiking.

On 4 February 1977, my thirtieth birthday, news of the granting of our visas for entry to Indonesia arrived and in Melbourne we immediately packed up and commenced our farewells and departure from Australia. We were excited to be leaving and completely unaware of the horrific drama unfolding in South Australia right at that time.

Sylvia Michelle Pittman was a sixteen-year-old shop assistant who had previously run away to Melbourne. Because of this, her parents, Andreas and Margerethe, had tried to give her more latitude, but wondered whether she had run away again when she failed to come home on Sunday 6 February 1977. Sylvia, however, had promised never to run away again, especially after being placed in a detention centre after the previous attempt. From her home in Taperoo, Sylvia had gone to see a friend who worked in a shop in the area, returned home and then gone out again. She was wearing her favourite medallion around her neck, given to her by her grandmother – this later became part of her identification. No witnesses emerged who saw her walking along the bus route towards the train station.

Vicki May Howell was older than the other girls were. A nurses' aide, she was twenty-six years old and the mother of two children. With a childhood spent in foster homes and constantly searching for the identity of her father, she lacked confidence and had been troubled as a young person. Married and then divorced, she was living with a young man called Harry on Anzac Highway, Kurralta Park. After an argument over a misunderstanding, Vicki packed her bag on 7 February 1977 and left. Because of her history of running away, she was not reported missing for several days, when her sister finally became worried. She was never seen again, and the stories of her last hours and what she wore are conflicting.

Connie Iordanides was sixteen years old and unemployed, and was known as Connie Jordan. Her childhood had been troubled and she had run away many times. Her father, Iordanis, believed that if the Department for Community Welfare had not interfered in their family life, then Connie might still be alive today. The family's bitter regrets about this issue made their anguish even more harrowing. On the night of Wednesday 9 February 1977, Connie left home to walk to her boyfriend's house about a kilometre away, so that they could go to the drive-in together. It is now believed that when she found her friend was not home, she headed into the city. Her parents say that they felt pressured by the DCW to give her more freedom than they might otherwise have done. They felt sure, however, that she did not intend to abscond that night, as she had made arrangements to meet a school friend the next day. She was never seen again.

Deborah Lamb, twenty years old, was also unemployed. Her parents, Ray and Rhonda, last heard from her about five months before she went out at about 6 p.m. on the night of 12 February 1977 from where she lived in the Windsor Gardens Caravan Park. Her relationship with them had been strained since they insisted that she hand over a baby for adoption, fearing that she could not care for it. Her parents did not know that she was missing for some time after this, but she was never seen after that night. According to the friend she shared the caravan with, she was most likely going to Hindley Street in the city, and probably hitchhiked as she had no other means of transport. Her caravan mate reported her missing when she did not return. After that night, she did not access her bank account nor claim her unemployment benefits. It would be many years later that her daughter, Nikki, in a search for her roots, would be shocked to discover the fate that had befallen her biological mother.

On that same day, 12 February, we boarded a Garuda flight in Sydney, heading for Jakarta, Indonesia, to catch a train to Bandung in West Java for the commencement of our Indonesian language course. We would live and work in various parts of Indonesia for the next decade. We took baby Naomi, and I was pregnant with our second child.

In just under seven weeks, seven young women, including Veronica, had vanished from the city streets of Adelaide. All were simply listed as missing persons and the reports joined the many hundreds of others filed away pending resolution. Three of them – Veronica, Vicki and Deborah – were over eighteen years of age and classified as adults. It is not a crime for an adult to disappear, and there are many reasons why people do.

Bruce Swanton sums up this question in his paper as follows:

> Seven girls had disappeared in seven weeks. Four of them had disappeared in the space of a week and yet it took two years before the South Australia Police realised a link between the disappearances and launched a full-scale investigation. Was the

delay in investigating a result of police attitudes to the victims when they were initially reported missing? Three of the women were unemployed, two of these were described as backward. Another two had histories of running away. Another was divorced and felt isolated and insecure. In her book Anne-Marie Mykyta describes her disbelief and disappointment at an editorial in *The Advertiser* which judged the victims and found them partly guilty of their eventual fate.

> ...girls who walk the streets at night, and are free with their favours, though they have the perfect right to do so, must realise that they are walking into mortal danger...[11]

It was wrong for the media to suggest that these women were 'free with their favours' when the only evidence they had was Miller's, who was convicted of six of the seven murders. The victims were clearly vulnerable, being females alone and on foot, but in no way could they be judged responsible for their own disappearances and deaths. Soon after Julie's disappearance, however, Anne-Marie Mykyta recalls her conversation with a police officer, when she reported Julie missing:

> 'Girls of that age are running off all the time. She'll be back when the novelty wears off.' But she wouldn't do this. 'If I had a dollar for every mother who's said that, I could retire from the police force... They get picked up in Victoria mostly, disturbing the peace or something like that; and the police there check out the missing persons file. You'll just have to wait.'[12]

And wait they did. In May 1979, after the bodies had finally been found, *The Advertiser* wrote that the police simply did not believe the families and thought that the girls had run away. That is often the assumption unless there is evidence of foul play, but clearly there was no outcry from the public, and the police response was minimal. Veronica would not have been saved, but the sobering possibility is that some or all of the other girls could have been. We will never know.

7

1977: An Accident

On 19 February 1977, Worrell and his girlfriend, Deborah Skuse, and Miller headed off in their car. The two men had been sleeping rough and had even had some interaction with the police. Debbie's plans to go away with a workmate to Kangaroo Island had fallen through and she had suggested that all three of them head off for a holiday weekend together. Deborah was a hairdresser and had managed to persuade Worrell to let her cut his long, glossy hair to shoulder length. After showing his new hairstyle to his approving mother, they climbed into the borrowed white Valiant and commenced their drive in the direction of Mount Gambier in the far east of South Australia, near the Victorian border.

After a couple of stops for food and petrol, they arrived in Mount Gambier in the early hours of Saturday morning and, feeling tired but not wanting to spend money, they all slept a while in the car. When he woke while the others kept sleeping, Miller then decided that he would drive them to Melbourne. He had second thoughts, however, after about a hundred kilometres when he realised that Worrell would be breaking his parole conditions by crossing the state border and going interstate without permission. So he drove back into South Australia and they looked around Mount Gambier and the famous Blue Lake, and did some shopping – buying a shotgun, of all things. Without warning, Worrell's demeanour changed. His mood darkened and Miller and Debbie wondered what had triggered it. Miller said in his account that he became anxious because Debbie was with them.

He knew very well what might have been about to occur. His concern, however, was apparently not sufficient to prevent him from picking up yet another female hitchhiker when they took a wrong route, ending up in Naracoorte. There is no record of where this girl left them.

As they finally headed for home, Miller became tired and asked Worrell to take over driving, in spite of the fact that Worrell had consumed at least three cans of beer and was still drinking while he drove a car with bald tyres and a defect notice from the police. It should be pointed out that one of Worrell's parole conditions was that he was not allowed to drink alcohol. Deborah became nervous as he drove erratically, and she complained. Miller felt the atmosphere darken again.

With an over-heating car engine, Worrell became angrier and sped on. Suddenly he yelled, 'We've got a blow-out!' as another car hurtled towards them.

Trying to avoid a collision, Worrell lost control and the car rolled over several times; Worrell and his girlfriend were thrown out of it before it came to a standstill, right way up. Miller crawled painfully out of the wrecked car to find the other two lying very still on the ground. Worrell had died instantly and his girlfriend died a little later. Miller was devastated, and wished he had died too, but he only sustained an injury to his shoulder.

Some friends drove down to the scene of the accident to take Miller back to Adelaide and he went to a friend's place to recuperate, where he found Worrell's ex-girlfriend, Amelia. She had only known Worrell a brief three weeks, but she too was very distressed. Miller decided to talk to her privately, so they went out to the backyard. The conversation that followed would turn out to be very significant some time later. Miller calls it 'the garden conversation' and asserts that it took place immediately after the accident and Worrell's death. Later at the trial, Amelia called it 'the kitchen conversation' and swore that it took place on the day of Worrell's funeral. This disparity of facts does not change the outcome of the event. This is Miller's account:

'Amelia, Chris had to die.'

'What do you mean?' she cried. 'Jamie, why did he have to die?'

I said, 'He just had to die. I wish I could tell you more but I don't want you to worry.'

'Please, Jamie, I must know.'

I then told her what I was to tell no one else before the trial. I said that Chris had done some really bad things, and he had to die for his own sake – he just had to die, I said. She continued asking why and I told her Chris had been killing girls and I knew because I had seen the girls after they were dead, I can show you where the bodies are. I said he had killed seven girls but that he could not help himself.[13]

What is clear is that Miller did tell Amelia, and that it is almost incomprehensible that she kept such explicit information about multiple murders to herself for over two years. Was she afraid of Miller, or even threatened by him? Did she discount the story as being a fanciful tale from a jealous friend of Worrell? Had she suspected something herself and was concerned that she had not reported it earlier? When the brief conversation was eventually made known to the police, it immediately directed the police search to James William Miller. Although it took place after the girls died, her information could have led to Miller directly, and, most importantly, brought the nightmare of the parents and families to an earlier conclusion. That may always remain a mystery.

8

1978: A Discovery

Swamp Road, Truro

It's quiet beside the road,
Swamp Road
Just past Truro.
Tree dotted red plains severed by the road
Scrubby bush creating dappled shade
Barbs on a harsh wire fence
Frogs croak from shallow pools of silence
Mosquitoes whine from the boggy spots
On the flood plain
Watered by the last rain
Five girls lie quietly
Hearing no more sounds
Not by choice
Their last decisions
Taking them towards the unmade road,
No coming back
From Swamp Road
Near Truro.
Long months of rest
Bird songs unheard and old mould layering
Seasons sliding past
Rain washing memories already gone
Just over the harsh fence
A little past Truro.

William Richard Thomas and his brother Rupert, of Nuriootpa, were looking for mushrooms in the bush beside Swamp Road, sixteen kilometres past the small town of Truro on 25 April 1978. Usually very dry, the area is a flood plain that springs to life after rains, activating the spores that lie latent in the baked earth. As they scanned the bushy area for the fungi they sought, they spotted what looked like the leg bone of a cow in some light scrub, but moved on, unaware of the significance of their find. According to their son Max, his mother, Valda, did not sleep well that night when she heard about the bones – the area is not a cattle-grazing area and has little pasture – and in a dream, she heard someone saying, 'Come, come.' That caused them to return together to the spot some days later to discover the remains of a young woman, including her shoe, some skin and painted nails, jeans and a jumper.

The remains were later identified as those of our Veronica, stumbled upon in her bush resting place after sixteen months of silence. There was no clear indication as to the cause of death, so, incredibly, it was assumed by some that she had become lost in the bush and died of thirst. Police reporter Rick Burnett wrote an article about the discovery, describing Veronica and her disappearance and mentioning the concern of her friends, church and hostel family. He concluded his article with the sentence

> Detectives Sergeant R. Thomas and Senior Constable R. Hunter, who are investigating, believe the circumstances are suspicious because Miss Knight had no reason to travel to Accommodation Hill, near Truro, where her remains were found. 'If the wallet was still with her it wouldn't be so suspicious,' Sen. Const. Hunter said.[14]

It is also worth noting that Veronica had no means of transport to get to the isolated and forsaken patch of bush well off the main road, and there do not seem to be any plausible suggestions about how she came to be there. The search for Veronica's remains extended nearly six hundred metres from the original discovery; what that search did not uncover, a mere hundred metres away across the dusty Swamp Road, were the remains of Vicki Howell and Connie Iordanides. Even when the disappearances of the girls were linked in mid-1978, there was no thorough search of the area. Nearly two years of lost time would pass by and no sounds broke the silence of the Truro scrub.

The letter arrived along with our assortment of mail. Even when marked 'Airmail', our mail followed the scenic route and could take ten days or even months – usually a plane to Jakarta and then a ship to the small town of Manokwari in West Papua, where we had been living and working for over a year. We always sorted our precious bundle of mail into family letters to be read first, other personal letters to read next, and then general mail, magazines and papers. The last ones were sorted into date order, to be savoured slowly and, hopefully, to last until the next ship berthed in our harbour and the next lot of mail arrived. Communication was slow but highly valued before the times of emails and without phone contact. West Papua is directly north of Australia but it might as well have been on another planet.

After we had devoured the family epistles with all their news, we started on the other letters. There was an air letter from Brian and Ruth, our Adelaide pastor friends. Anticipating interesting news from them about their family and our friends, we slit it open. I almost stopped breathing as we read the opening lines in Ruth's handwriting. She was writing to tell us that they had sad news to share with us: Veronica's body had been found in the bush. Time stopped still for a moment as the terrible truth sank in. Our lovable young friend was dead, and possibly had been since before the day when Peter looked for her on the train. Although we had always suspected that something had happened to her, the reality was shocking and made me feel physically ill. How had she died? We sat on the side of our bed together and sobbed in disbelief in our delayed grief. We would never see Veronica again. She would never meet Naomi.

In South Australia, Brian and Ruth's elder daughter had gone to the corner shop in Port Lincoln where she was living and saw the headlines on the front page of the paper announcing the discovery of Veronica's body. Shocked and aghast that her parents had not warned her about this terrible news, she phoned them only to discover that she was breaking the news to them as well. The ripples began to spread out and had now reached us in West Papua.

We held each other as our emotions and thoughts poured out until we were spent, and then I looked up at the wall. In our bedroom was an orange fabric banner – a precious memento made for us by the Bart's Club children when we left Adelaide. We valued it so much that it was hanging in pride of place in the bedroom, where we could see it all the time. And right at the top, in childish scrawl, was Veronica's message: 'The Lord is my Shepherd I shall not want. Psalm 23.1. Veronica Knight.' We hugged each other more tightly and felt a peace creep in and sit next to our sadness as we remembered that she knew the Good Shepherd and was safe with him. She was one of the world's nobodies –

apparently no supportive family, limited education and few prospects for the future; none of that, however, was her fault. In God's eyes, she was a precious lamb.

    We both knew in that moment the supernatural comfort of God's grace and love. This, however, in no way diminished the pain in the months that followed, as the devastating extent of what had been perpetrated against Veronica and six other young women began to unfold.

9

1978: A Funeral

Veronica left a very light footprint. Her belongings at the Sutherland Lodge Hostel were collected by Brian and stored at the church. She owned very little – a sewing machine, kept in the storeroom, was her most valuable possession. Her photo album contains just fifty-six photos and one newspaper cutting. There is a strip of photos taken in a photo booth on another occasion with a friend called Raymond. She looks happy, just as she would have on that last night, like any girl who has been shopping for clothes, is with a friend and is anticipating an interstate trip. That is the way we want to remember her.

On 11 December 1978, Veronica was buried at the North Brighton Cemetery in a brief service led by the Reverend Brian Fagan. F.H. Trevelion & Son were the funeral directors. It is possible that a half-sibling attended the funeral, but there are no records. In the funeral book of St Bartholomew's Anglican Church (now kept at St Matthew's, Kensington), it says,

> Disappeared 23/12/76 – body found earlier this year; murder suspected.

I found a photograph of her headstone on the internet and gazed at it a long time. This is her 'Allambi', the 'resting place' now of her physical remains. Had she not been killed, she would have been sixty this year, and that is hard for me to imagine. She never had the chance to grow up and for us she will always be eighteen and full of life. Not even her dates of birth and death are noted on the simple headstone:

the short time she was with us is not recorded for history and will be quickly forgotten. Rest in peace ,Veronica – nothing can harm you now.

For Veronica

1958
Her birth unsung
Unnoticed
A life begun unheralded
Unseen
Into the system
Foster home,
Foster parents,
Foster families,
Mother gone from life
Father wasting life
Nothing to give to Veronica.

Learning struggles
Life battles
Love in deficit, craved but gone.
Given up to the State
A ward, a file card
A disability
Homes and hostels
Identity forgotten.
Veronica who?
When?

1976
Evil roams the streets
Snaring the naïve
Snatching her away
On the lonely, dark road to Truro.

In the white car
A cowardly Valiant
Not the love she craved
Just black hurt and hell before her death.
Flung lifeless into the scrub
Covered lightly
Leaves and twigs
Forgotten.

1978
Random stumbling on remains
And a shoe
Lost girl in every way
Never looked for.
Others snatched and destroyed
Families devastated, waiting
While Veronica was forgotten.

1980
Evil halted
Justice sought
Families grieving
For all but Veronica
Convictions given
For the lives of six others
Except Veronica.
Who?

10

1979: A Search

Meanwhile the Mykyta family, like all the families, had tried to move on with their lives, with no news of their daughter, Julie. An important turning point occurred on 22 January 1979; a plain-clothes police officer, Detective Sergeant Bob Giles, came to visit Mr and Mrs Mykyta.

'We have reason to believe that your daughter might have met with foul play.'

'Why now? It's been nearly two years.'

'It is exactly two years today,' Irush said suddenly.

'Your daughter is missing, Mrs Mykyta. In spite of our efforts' – he held up one hand as if to stop me from speaking – 'and we have made efforts, believe me, we can find no trace of her. When a person goes missing, we can usually find something, someone has seen her, or heard about her. But here, we have your daughter, she goes into King William Street to catch a bus, and she's never heard of again.'

'But it's been so long. I didn't think…I mean, we didn't hear.'

'Well, there's no point in coming to you and saying we can't find anything, is there? We deal with a lot of missing persons, and most of them turn up pretty quickly. Besides it's a question of how far we ought to go; being a missing person is not a crime, you know… What we have to find out is whether she disappeared of her own volition… But now it's not just Julie.'

'But what made you think…?'

'I'm attached to Missing Persons at the moment. And I got out the files and started looking through them. And there's your daughter, she's been missing two years, and then there's another little girl, came up from the south coast in a bus, probably walked down

King William street to get a bus home. She's been missing two years. And the girl, Veronica Knight; she was waiting in King William Street to get a bus home, and she disappeared two years ago.'

'She's the one they found in the paddock last year,' I murmured.

'That's right. We don't know how she died, but we are starting to get very worried.' He leaned forward. 'Now what I have to tell you, Mrs Mykyta, Mr Mykyta, is that we've got five little girls, possibly more, who have disappeared in the same way.'

I stared at him. 'No...no...no.'[15]

The police had a request of the Mykyta family. None of the other parents had been willing to expose their family tragedy to media and public spotlight, but it was felt that it was time to make a plea for information. Nothing else was working and the cases had long gone cold.

'I want you to give an interview to the press. I've arranged for a reporter from *The News* to come and see you. I just want you to talk about Julie and what you think might have happened to her. Will you do that?'

'Yes, of course. And the other parents?'

He looked away, a faint trace of embarrassment in his face. 'Well, the other parents aren't all in a position...I mean, it's very difficult for some people...'

'All right,' I said. 'We'll see the reporter. We'll do our best.'[16]

Two articles were subsequently published in *The News* and *The Advertiser*.

'NUMBER THREE GIRL STILL MISSING: Is Julie a murder victim?' screamed the headlines of the article in Adelaide's afternoon tabloid newspaper on 24 January.[17] Mr and Mrs Mykyta had reluctantly submitted to being interviewed so that the public could be alerted to the fact that their daughter was still missing. It seemed to them that there was now no other explanation but foul play, and they also wanted to talk about the disappearance 'as a warning to other young girls'. They spoke of the emotional see-saw that their lives had become, and asserted that their daughter 'was a good girl'. When she read the article in the paper the next day, Mrs Mykyta felt that those quoted words made her sound like a prude and regretted giving the interview – nothing was ever easy. Mr Mykyta reassured her that it didn't matter, as long as the news was out there and awareness raised. Soon after this, the mother of Tania Kenny phoned her and they found some common ground in their suffering.

Although the area was searched at the time of Veronica's discovery, it was to be another year later on Easter Sunday, April 1979, before the skeletal remains of Sylvia Pittman, a Taperoo shop assistant, were found in the same area where Veronica had been discovered. Four bushwalkers out shooting rabbits accidentally came across Sylvia's remains in the bush and she was identified by dental records and a fourteen-carat gold medallion necklet of a guardian angel, the treasured gift from her Austrian grandmother in 1970. Her parents saw it shown on TV and recognised it – such a terrible moment of realisation for them.

We had pressed on with our lives in West Papua, but things came to a halt around that time when I discovered a lump in my breast. On advice, and because I was also pregnant again, I travelled back to Australia in April 1979 for medical treatment and had tests in Sydney to set my mind at rest. While I was staying with my aunt and uncle, we were watching TV one evening, right at the time when the shocking news item of the finding of Sylvia's body was announced. My diary records,

> ...the discovery of more remains of a girl, in the same paddock as Veronica was found in (three other girls who were missing at that time are suspected to have been killed by the same person). Veronica's photo and story were shown, and Mike Willesee featured the story in his programme. I sat there with tears in my eyes as they showed the paddock where she was found. But I was glad I saw it. Who would kill someone like Veronica? Praise the Lord she is safe from it all now. 19 April 1979

It was such an amazing coincidence that I was in Australia at the time of the discovery and the subsequent TV show, but it was hard to process the awful news on my own. I did not want to distress my uncle and aunt, who had no connection with Veronica, and I felt so far from Peter and my family. We managed a very short phone call that night, but were mainly overcome with the relief of the good outcome of my medical tests and I didn't feel as if I could talk to Peter about the news I had just seen – the call was expensive. That night I cried in bed, a blubbery mix of relief after the day's medical events, grief for the Veronica and the other family, and simply feeling very alone when my home and loved ones were in distant West Papua.

On that day, the newspapers in Adelaide published articles describing the finding of the two bodies and suggesting that there may be more. The article in *The Advertiser* was accompanied by a photograph of Julie Mykyta, and some statistics concerning missing persons.

Sergeant Bob Giles (affectionately known as 'Hugger') had realised that there might be a pattern to the happenings, and had been working on the files of missing persons from around the same time. He had expected the second skeleton to be Julie Mykyta, after the public campaign to find her, but he had come up with the names of four other young women who disappeared around the same time and who until then were assumed to be 'voluntary absent'. There was now a total of seven girls, and the largest murder investigation in the state's history had begun. This was the very first time that the pattern of disappearances had been tracked, but the mystery was why they had suddenly stopped after 12 February 1977.

Detective Ken Thorsen, who retired in 1987, was officer-in-charge of the then Major Crime Squad when the Truro investigation was launched.

> 'I can vividly remember the moment when Sergeant Bob Giles, who is now deceased, brought the seven missing persons reports into my office,' he said. 'We went through each one carefully and then both came to the same conclusion. We realised then there had been a serial killer operating in Adelaide and the inquiry was launched after discussions with then police commissioner Laurie Draper.' Mr Thorsen said he appointed now retired detectives Glen Lawrie and Peter Foster as the primary investigation team.[18]

Lawrie and Foster began their painstaking work – they compared similarities between the victims and the way they disappeared, their ages and other characteristics. They also moved into a new area of investigation – psychological profiling of the perpetrator.

> The detectives decided the perpetrator was most likely to be a man who lived in Adelaide, probably in an inner suburb, who was a sex offender who'd spent time in prison. They thought that he had probably been released prior to the first murder, and that the series had ceased because he was back in prison.[19]

A further search by the police for the death of known criminals by suicide or accident around that time finally brought up the name of Christopher Worrell, who had been killed on 19 February 1977, along with his girlfriend, Deborah Skuse, in a car accident – a week after the last disappearance on 12 February. Suddenly the jigsaw pieces started to fit and the inexplicable began to make sense; the hunt was on. It had taken two years, but finally the police were confident enough to develop an action plan to try, once again, to draw out some facts that would lead them to what they were beginning to suspect would be a tragic saga.

Detective Thorsen also noted in *The Sunday Mail*, on the occasion of Miller's death in prison in 2008,

> ...the shortcomings in SAPOL's procedures that allowed the seven women to be abducted and murdered without the pattern being detected had 'long been' changed.
>
> 'You could never rule it out, but it's likely a pattern would be picked up fairly quickly today when compared with back then,' he said. 'Missing persons reporting is a problem for police throughout the world, but the way it is managed here ensures patterns are picked up quickly now.'[20]

I returned from my medical trip to Sydney back to our simple home in West Papua, relieved that I had been cleared of my health concerns, happy to get back to our family life and ready to prepare for the birth of our third child. I told Peter about the Willesee program I had seen on TV in Australia and we were saddened to think of another family's sorrow at the discovery of another body – their daughter. We had no way of gaining more information and just had to move on from our grief at Veronica's terrible death.

In spite of the extensive search around the area where Veronica was found, the police hunt at that time missed finding any other remains. The accidental finding of Sylvia Pittman, and Bob Giles' work on an emerging pattern,

> had the effect of throwing the investigation into top gear. Giles' original theory looked more likely than ever, and Thorsen called for help from the recently formed South Australian Police specialist section known as STAR force. At first his call for help was denied on the grounds that STAR force was about to carry out a major training exercise, but Thorsen went into bat with the commissioner and got everything he asked for.[21]

A massive search was launched. This operation was the biggest of its kind in SA police history, and involved nearly ninety personnel, including sixty cadets. They camped in primitive conditions in the parched clay paddocks of the Truro area with instructions to comb a section of nearly twenty square kilometres that covered where the four bodies had been found. It stretched from the Sturt Highway in

the north to Sandleton Road in the south and from Halfway House Road in the east across Swamp Road and beyond. The sixty cadets were in a line, each five metres apart, and searched the eastern end of the area. The search was difficult and the conditions unpleasant and challenging, but they pressed on.

In addition, police on horseback and the dog squad also assisted with the search, concentrating on the western side of Swamp Road. Inspector Sampson addressed the men and spurred them on as the operation dragged on with no further result. It is said that some personnel had only two hours of sleep in three days.

Finally, on 26 April 1979, resulting from the police search, two more bodies were found by the mounted police, only a hundred metres across Swamp Road from where Veronica had been dumped. The site was clearly visible from the road. They were the remains of Vicki May Howell, twenty-six, who was married and left two children, and Connie Iordanides, fifteen. They were forensically identified, and that brought finality and more sadness for two more families.

In early May in 1979, the police were working manually through hundreds and thousands of files cards for reports of attempted abductions of young women or anyone who remembered being offered a lift, on the basis that the perpetrators would have approached many more apart from their eventual victims. Anne-Marie Mykyta articulated her pain as the now very public search went on, with four bodies found but as yet no sign of Julie.

> The search went on. Night after night. The news seemed to be full of those flat, empty paddocks; the long line of policemen only emphasised the desolation. Marko and I watched it all. If I was out of the room when something came on, he would call urgently. We were mesmerised. Wherever we turned there was reference to the search; if we turned away, the search went on in our minds. There was nothing in the world but Julie…Julie…Julie.[22]

And so there was still no closure for the Mykyta family. Anne-Marie had heard that more bodies had been found, and although she did not want one of them to be Julie, the agony of not knowing was too much for her. It was all overwhelming for her after the long wait and she even considered ending it all.

> That night was the dark night of my soul. I lay in bed, staring into the darkness, and decided I could not bear to live any longer… I thought of the doctors I knew, and wondered if they would give me sleeping pills. They probably would, under the circumstances… There would be an end to the struggle…and I could just let go… My plans were made.[23]

Anne-Marie makes no claims to have Christian faith, but that night she was supported by those who did. She woke up feeling surprisingly stronger and thought of the ones who would miss her. What she didn't know, but found out later was that an educational aide in her school who was a believer, had organised a hundred people to pray that night that she would have strength through it all. The miracle happened and she woke up with new courage to face what was ahead.

The police had not pursued the search in mid-1978 when the disappearance of the first five girls was linked, and did not request the Mykyta family to publicise their loss until January in 1979. Bob Whitington and Peter de Ionno of *The Advertiser* interviewed over forty people connected to the case in preparation for a major article that appeared in *The Saturday Review* on 12 May. They concluded that

> Police believed that Mykyta, Knight and Pittman had run away. The girls' parents and friends did not believe this. Police made no statement about the five linked disappearances until after Sylvia Pittman's skeleton was accidentally found by bushwalkers on Easter Sunday. Once the conclusion that they were dealing with a multiple killer was inescapable they began organising thorough searches which quickly uncovered the third and fourth bodies… The two biggest obstacles to the solution of the case are two years of lost time coupled with public indifference to the slayings. Outrage and a hue and cry for the killer are noticeably absent.[24]

11

2018: A Mounted Police Officer

Am I ever going to finish writing this book? A key player from the saga so long ago has emerged and I have a phone number to call – it is Harry, the mounted police officer who was part of the famous search. By an astounding coincidence, he is the father-in-law of Nicola, the family tracing coordinator in Adelaide who has helped me trace significant people – and she discovered Harry's role in it all. What will he be able to tell me about the search in the Truro bush? What was it like to be part of the biggest search in police history in South Australia? I imagine that if there are some experiences one never forgets, this must be one of them. I thought I had most of the facts of this story assembled, but this is a first-hand account that no one else can tell. I cannot believe that I have made contact with him.

I call his number at the arranged time, and we talk like old friends for three-quarters of an hour. I had a list of questions to ask but he jumps right in and opens with 'It was pretty confronting.'

I try to imagine the memories and images he is calling up as he begins to speak. From time to time, he addresses interested gatherings about the period of the murders and the part he played, so that has kept the memory alive for him. No doubt, the visual images have stayed with him too.

Veronica's remains were found in April 1978, Sylvia's in April 1979 and now Harry was part of the search that followed in May 1979 for others who were believed to be buried in Truro. The enormous search in the Truro bush that captured the horrified imagination of South

Australia and the nation was focused on a barren patch of scrub north of Adelaide.

'Tell me about the camp and how you were organised,' I ask, because I have tried to imagine what it was like for ninety police to camp in the dusty scrub.

It was unseasonally hot for autumn that year, but there was also rain to contend with, so the conditions were challenging for the men. The well-trained mounted police had the additional responsibility of caring for their hard-working horses – feeding and watering them and making sure they were not overworked.

Harry talks about the three days he spent on the search with about sixteen mounted police out in the bush, and how the horse floats, equipped with bunks, doubled as sleeping quarters for the police riders. Once the horses were at the site and out of the floats, there were four bunk beds for the police, and another couple could sleep in the front, with extra stretchers in another float at the back. Four men made up each section and there were four sections deployed for this search.

Harry led a team made up of Sarge, Mick and John, and they worked closely together. He knows the dog squad officers were out there too, but didn't see them as they were on the other side of the road – the eastern side where the first two bodies were found – with each group concentrating on their allocated area. There was a bit of feeling around the troops that the high-profile mounted police were photographed more often than the others were, but nobody could deny that the beautiful, well-trained horses were photogenic and looked good in the papers. The public wanted to know that all resources were being deployed to solve this terrible mystery.

He remembers that the newly formed STAR force (Special Task and Rescue, the police tactical group in South Australia) organised them all into different areas and gave them their orders. There were police cadets and police officers on motorbikes as well. It took them most of the first day to set up camp and make organisational decisions, and then the search was really under way. Harry thinks it was the second day when they were heading back from their dusty work at lunchtime. He suggested to Chief Superintendent Dennis Edmonds (known as 'Smoothy'), 'Why don't we pull up, and stand on the fence to hold it down while we lead the four horses carefully over the barbed wire and then spread out and have a look here before we break for lunch?'

It was 1.50 p.m. when he found it – a three-by-two-foot grave, just roughly covered up in the bush with a huge branch lying over the top where it had dropped. Harry immediately called it in over the radio and the media and STAR force men came quickly to join them. Harry tells me how he was on the lookout for some platform shoes while searching – they knew that one of the girls had been wearing them. He comments that his wife had some, so he knew what they were and that brought it close to home. Somehow, there were two kinds of feelings: satisfaction at finding what they were looking for, and horror and sadness at the confronting nature of human remains.

The STAR force expected the constables to do the heavy work and handed them the shovels to start digging. The men sweated in the heat, still stunned that they had found what they were out there for. So many searches reveal nothing after long hours of hard work, but today they had a result that was going to be sad for some families.

Harry describes how they delayed lunch to keep searching, feeling that they were now in the right area. Over two years after they disappeared, the final resting places of these girls had been found. Now sixty-eight and a great-grandfather, Harry will never forget that day; it is seared in his memory.

He urged his men on to keep looking and only a hundred metres or so further on and ten minutes later, he saw what they were looking for. There were many kangaroo bones out there in the bush but he knew they had made another find, and these weren't animal remains. The almost intact remains, complete with a single platform shoe, were a fourth body in the Truro bush.

'I think we have another one.' He dismounted carefully, making sure he didn't disturb the crime scene. Although it was early days for forensic science, dental records (for five girls) and, later, craniofacial video superimposition would be used to speed up the formal identification as the families waited anxiously – wanting to know the identity of the bodies but dreading the truth that would take away their last hopes for their daughters.[25]

I ask Harry about his career path. When he left school at seventeen, he went straight to the Police Academy for his three years of training. One day while he was still a teenager, he was run over by a car when he was walking home and had major surgery on his leg, and the scars are still there today. Nevertheless, he was able to pursue his career as a mounted police officer until 1986, when he moved to the radar and random breath testing unit, but he did not enjoy the shift work and called it a day for policing. He has changed his career path completely and trained to work with the Salvation Army.

And so it was that Senior Sergeant Dennis Edmonds (in charge of the Major Crime Squad) called in the discovery of the fourth body in the Truro bush.

The media had all gone home apart from journalist Bert Stansbury from *The News*, who said, 'This is all mine now,' and began to take some photos.

Connie and Vicki had been found at last, over two years after they disappeared. Harry tells me that he lost his appetite for the barbecue lunch that had been prepared for his men. Now, forty years later, we are both thoughtful as we reflect on how the tragedy unfolded over those next three weeks.

12

1979: An Arrest

James Miller had continued to be as obsessed with Christopher Worrell after his accidental death as before his friend died. He had posted a memorial paragraph in February 1978 in *The Advertiser* on the anniversary of his death, which read,

> Worrell, Christopher Robin. Memories of a very close friend who died 12 months ago this week. Your friendship, your thoughtfulness and kindness, Chris, will always be remembered by me, mate. What comes after death I can hope, as I pray we meet again.[26]

No one posted a memorial for Veronica.

At that time, we had finally arrived in West Papua after a year at Indonesian language school in Bandung in West Java. We were staying in temporary accommodation in the bay-side town of Manokwari, waiting to move into the house on the main street that we would rent and renovate. A long way away from any news and life in Australia, we heard only what we received in letters from our family and friends – usually quite a time after the event – and occasional news on our radio that picked up Radio Australia. A year after her death, Veronica had not even been found or given a proper burial.

Somehow over the years, we absorbed the tragedy of losing her, but did not think of her anniversaries or feel connected enough to reflect on our loss as time went by. We didn't even remember her birthday. Our life half a degree south of the equator was busy and involving for us and we were fully extended in our work and parenting our two small children. On top of that, in 1979 I was coping with the two toddlers and a pregnancy in the tropics and day-long nausea. I had no energy to think any more widely than of the demands of living in our primitive part of the world. With a kerosene burner for cooking, no electricity and only the rainwater we collected, life was basic and hard in the sweaty heat of our town by the water. Intermittent bouts of malaria assaulted us all, with the side effects from medications sometimes worse than the disease. My goal was to get through each day, support my husband in his teaching job, feed my family, raise my kids and fall into bed each night with a mosquito net for protection from malarial mosquitoes. Our Australian connection seemed a long way away.

In contrast, back in Australia, the unfolding drama of the Truro story was front-page news in Adelaide and all over the nation. *The West Australian* in Perth – a long way away from Adelaide – featured the search on its front page on 27 April, detailing the finding of the third and fourth bodies by the mounted police, supported by graphic photos.[27] In May 1979, with no further revelations or discoveries, a reward was posted of $30,000, made up of $20,000 from the government and an additional $10,000 from *The Advertiser* – a large sum of money at that time. An amnesty was offered by the police to anyone with information who wasn't directly involved in the murders, but Miller knew that his degree of involvement would be a moot point.

He felt the net closing in and wondered whether Amelia, Worrell's ex-girlfriend, would take her secrets to the police. He claimed that he could not give up the information for the sake of Worrell's mother – he didn't want her to suffer any more. Bizarrely, however, he did not feel this same compassion for the mothers of the missing girls. They and the families waited, each day of emptiness depleting their stores of hope and making it less and less likely that their daughters would return to them. No parent, however, gives up until all hope is extinguished.

Miller chronicles in his rather selective account that he was drifting and began to be afraid as the hunt intensified. Once the second body was found, the media began to print lists of missing girls and when and where they were last seen. The police publicised the fact that they were seeking a criminal with a history of violence – Miller was well aware that he would soon be connected with Worrell, who fitted the profile as well as the timing of the murders – and that the killer could be dead. The search was gaining momentum and Miller knew it would only be a matter of time before the police would draw some accurate conclusions.

> I could feel that a net must be closing around me but to leave town then would only succeed in having a warrant sworn out for my arrest…No way I wanted to be securely locked up in prison for police to easily find me if they came looking… At this time police were offering a free pardon for anyone with information who wasn't directly involved with the actual murders…It was true that I only helped Chris get rid of the bodies but would they give me a free pardon if I came forward? I doubted it very much.[28]

The reward was increased to a total of $40,000, and that finally drew out an informant who led the police to 'Angela', as she was known then; her name was actually Amelia – Worrell's ex-girlfriend. She was finally persuaded to speak to the police – probably by the unnamed person who collected the reward – and shared the explicit information she had been hiding for all that time. The detective task force now had all they needed to track down Miller, and they wasted no time.

> Angela defended herself for not passing her information on to the police earlier on the grounds that Worrell was dead. She said that she was opposed to 'dobbing in' anyone, a truly Australian characteristic, and feared Miller would become a scapegoat for Worrell's crimes.[29]

Significantly, Worrell fitted perfectly the profile of the killer that Lawrie and Foster had drawn up, and when it was discovered that his death in the car crash was consistent with the time frame and provided a reason why the killing frenzy was halted, it all began to make sense to the police.

Miller was of no fixed address at that time and did some work daily at the Adelaide Central Mission (known as the Derelict Centre) for a little cash before heading out to find a place to sleep on the street each night. He was to discover later that eight police officers had been assigned to track him down on 23 May 1979. Miller glanced out of the window while he was working and saw a female sitting in a car and became nervous, deciding to go outside and test to see if she showed interest in him. She did. He tried to leave the building but was apprehended and taken to the police headquarters. The chase was over and James William Miller was finally in custody.

While that day's edition of *The Women's Weekly* had a cover title of 'Ten Golden Rules for Family Happiness', the lives of a number of deeply saddened Adelaide families were about to be shocked by the revelations that would emerge.

At the police station in Angas Street, not far from Veronica's last place of residence, Miller was interviewed by detectives Glen Lawrie and Peter Foster. They took turns and typed up the interview as they went. After having now read the transcript of the interview relevant to Veronica, I cannot imagine that it is a verbatim account, but rather a record of what was remembered when the interviewer left the room for the other one to take over. Miller claimed that he asked for a solicitor, but the police say that was not the case.

Miller talked freely (and, according to the police, loosely with regard to the truth). Even his own story in his book differs from what he told the police that night. There are many discrepancies – among them, whether Worrell threatened Miller with a knife, which is in the book but not mentioned to the police.

In the interview, Miller says that Veronica was killed at Truro, but in his book, he describes taking her to the hills, where she was killed, and then driving her body to Truro. He notes in his book that he threw her handbag away into a drain and that Worrell took the money, but in the interview he simply says they threw it away in the northern suburb of Elizabeth. Miller actually states in his book that he lied to the police and made up stories in his interview because he was annoyed that he did not get a solicitor.[30] For whatever reason, it is impossible to verify many of the things he said in his interview, his unsworn statement later in court and then in his book. The only clear fact is that there are numerous discrepancies and that he frequently contradicted his own account.

The talking went on into the night until the police became exasperated and Commander Thorsen says that he called a halt to take Miller to the cells. At that stage, he should have been charged, bailed or taken to court in the morning. Miller then dramatically turned things around by offering to take them to find the remaining bodies. He claims that he had nothing to lose and sincerely believed that he would not be charged with murder.

What a dilemma for the police! They knew that the correct procedure should be followed so that the case would stand up in court, yet clearly Miller would be likely to say no more once he had a solicitor and was charged. The families' extended nightmare was uppermost in their minds and they decided to make what Thorsen calls a 'bold decision' for the sake of the parents: they would take Miller out immediately that evening and find the bodies, and trust that the court would understand and allow the decision to stand. The other important factor was that they still had no forensic evidence apart from Amelia's information to connect Miller to the murders. A confession would help, but locating the remains would make their case rock solid, and so they felt that the risk they took was worthwhile.

The dramatic night expedition took place in frosty conditions. Thorsen, Lawrie and Foster took Miller and met a team of other police and forensic experts at Truro. There were even journalists present who had somehow got wind of the breaking story and obtained dramatic and graphic photos of the event, which was starkly lit by the headlights of cars. Miller led them unerringly to the fifth and last body that was buried at Truro, several kilometres from where the other four graves were located, off a dirt road leading to a farmhouse. His ability to find the secluded grave on that dark night in the scrub left no doubt concerning his involvement in the crimes. It would turn out to be the resting place of Julie Mykyta, ending the long agony of waiting for her family. She was fully clothed and still had money stuffed in her jeans pocket. After they all left the site, 'Only footprints remained in the frosty paddock.'[31] The police had enough evidence now to charge Miller with four murders, including Veronica's.

Unable to find the last two bodies that night, the entourage had to return the next day to Wingfield to find the remains of Tania Kenny and then proceed to Port Gawler, where fifty police searched and eventually, on 29 May, found Deborah Lamb's body in a deep grave, bound in a wood and iron box.

After formal identification had taken place, mainly using dental charts, the seven families devastated by this horrific event knew that their girls would never come home. All hope had gone with the retrieval of the bodies and each family began their own journey of grief and soul-searching and tried to find a way into a new but sad future. Knowledge of their daughters' fates brought clarity but took their distress to a new level and would affect the course of the rest of their lives. Even in the light of the discovery of the last bodies, Anne-Marie Mykyta struggled.

> I could not believe she was dead: it must all have been a hideous mistake.[32]

13

The 1970s: Forgotten

Veronica Knight and James Miller were both products of a government system that treated disadvantaged children very badly, although we have no records of either Veronica's or Miller's experiences. After each being placed in a number of homes, reformatories or institutions, their lives crossed very briefly but violently in a tragic manner in 1976; their actions on that fateful night were both in some way shaped towards being either a victim or a criminal by their respective backgrounds in institutions.

There is a whole generation of forgotten children who became wards of the state in the 1960s and 1970s. To make for a confusing history, government homes in South Australia have come under a long series of jurisdictions and continually changing departments: Destitute Persons Department – The Destitute Board, 1849–1886, the State Children's Department – State Children's Council, 1886–1927, Children's Welfare and Public Relief Department, 1927–1966, Aborigines Protection Board, 1934–1963, Department of Aboriginal Affairs, 1963–1970, Department of Social Welfare, 1966–1970, Department of Social Welfare and Aboriginal Affairs, 1970–1972, Department for Community Welfare, 1972–1990 and Department of Family and Community Services, 1990–1998. The current relevant department is Children, Youth and Family Services, 1999–present. To track down any one child's history during any of these periods is extremely difficult and many records never existed in the first place or have subsequently been lost or destroyed.

As a friend – but not an immediate relative – of Veronica, I found it impossible to glean any definitive information about her earlier history at all. My attempts to enquire through Find and Connect, the Australian government project set up to help people find their histories, met a stonewall. As the service says at the head of a page on disability homes,

> The links between children's institutions and disability institutions in all states and territories mean that these Homes are part of the history of the Forgotten Australians.[33]

When we first met Veronica, we were told that she was 'handicapped', as was the description in those days. She struggled with reading and writing, and her experiences had been limited to institutional life. At the same time, we noticed that she was usually quick to understand, could connect well with people and was able to care for herself in her rather limited environment. Her contact with the church and us extended her circle of friends and expanded her experience, and we felt that she had potential that had not yet been tapped. Although we had no official diagnosis or testing to go by, we did not think that she was truly disabled. We do know that Veronica attended a special school as a child, and that probably limited her development. She was assessed as being capable only of working at Bedford Industries, a workplace for the disabled, and thus limits were placed on her future.

As far as I know, Veronica's mother died when she was very young and her father was an alcoholic, so she was handed over as a baby to be cared for by the state. She may or may not have been in foster homes in her infancy, but we do know that as a young child, she was placed in Minda Home in Brighton North, and the few photographs that remain of her life show some friends and connections there. Minda used to be called 'Home for the Weak Minded' in an earlier era and it is true that many wards of the state were judged to be disabled and, once classified as such, were inexorably set on their life path of disadvantage. Even today, the word 'Minda', when used in Adelaide, is actually a term used insultingly, the equivalent of the way 'retard' used to be used offensively. It was a lifelong derogatory label.

Forgotten Australians could be incorrectly diagnosed as being 'feeble-minded' or 'mentally defective' and be placed in a disability Home. The 'dull' characteristics that led to these false classifications were often the result of abuse and neglect, sometimes from the very institutions supposed to be 'caring' for them.[34]

Veronica had photos in her album of someone – Shirley – she labelled as a sister, but to my knowledge she had no contact with her in the time we knew her and we never met a family member. It often happened that families were split up and never reunited, adding to the loss of identity and the label of 'forgotten Australians'. Not knowing or having no contact with a person's family context is part of the struggle to form one's identity and history – the right of every human. In a practical sense, it means there is no knowledge of medical history or congenital family issues, and that can have an impact on later generations.

> The long term impact of a childhood spent in institutional care is complex and varied. However, a fundamental, ongoing issue is the lack of trust and security and lack of interpersonal and life skills that are acquired through a normal family upbringing, especially social and parenting skills.
>
> A lifelong inability to initiate and maintain stable, loving relationships was described by many Forgotten Australians who have undergone multiple relationships and failed marriages. Many cannot form trust in relationships and remain loners, never marrying or living an isolated existence…

The legacy of their childhood experiences for far too many has been low self-esteem, lack of confidence, depression, fear and distrust, anger, shame, guilt, obsessiveness, social anxieties, phobias, and recurring nightmares. Many care leavers have tried to block the pain of their past by resorting to substance abuse through life-long alcohol and drug addictions. Many turned to illegal practices such as prostitution, or more serious law-breaking offences which have resulted in a large percentage of the prison population being care leavers.[35]

When she reached the age limit at Minda Home, Veronica moved in 1974 to Allambi, where we met her for the first time. At sixteen, she had finished at her special school and began some work with Bedford Industries. Institutionalisation has the effect of narrowing options and life directions, and it does not seem as though anyone was thinking about her long-term welfare. The girls at Allambi became her family, and she benefited enormously from being part of the community at the church. Everyone who remembers Veronica says that she was friendly and fun to be with; her expanded social circle was good for her developing social awareness and provided a life outside the institution.

After we left for Melbourne in 1976, Veronica was on the move again. No one can remember the reason now, but she needed to move from Allambi, possibly because it was closing or was to be used for another purpose. Our good friends Brian and Ruth took her in to stay with them for most of the month of June that year, so for the first time in her life, Veronica was part of a functional family with four other teenage children. Ruth remembers happy times around the large rectory dining table and Veronica fitting in well with the family. They showed great kindness to Veronica and she was able to be fully involved in the church activities that she enjoyed.

Her next movements are not remembered by anyone still alive, but we know that she went to live with a lady who needed a live-in companion while her regular girl was away. Once again, there was apparently no plan for any career for Veronica, who would probably not have been paid but worked for free board in that home while still doing some work. It is not clear now who made these decisions, but her greatest need was to have somewhere secure to live. When the previous girl returned as the lady's companion, the two girls did not get on so well, and her employer contacted Sutherland Lodge Salvation Army Hostel for Girls to ask if they had room for her.

The hostel (now a rooming house) was at 341 Angas Street near the city and had forty-two young women who were working or studying in the area and needed somewhere to stay. The matron called them together to ask how they felt about having a disabled person moving in with them and the vote was unanimous – Veronica could come. She would be the first of a few girls working at Bedford Industries who would stay at the lodge, including her friend Jenny. Matron Reed worked around the clock, day in, day out, to look after the girls and she felt personally responsible for them. Up early every day, she cooked their breakfast to give them a good start to the day, and made sure that they were all home safe each night. She

had minimal assistance for this demanding job, but loved those girls like they were her own family. She remembers Veronica as a girl with zest for life. The girls could come and go as they pleased but were expected, like in any family, to phone if they were staying out for the night or running late. Veronica spent her last day in an institution, after only ten weeks of living at Sutherland Lodge. Veronica's disadvantages followed her to the end of her short life. When she disappeared, she was not missed by many and had little significant attention paid to her case. She was perceived as a state ward with an institutional background, and that led to assumptions about why she had disappeared that were not based on facts. Her main advocate was the matron who reported her missing and returned frequently to the police station asking for news. With little information available or sought and the Christmas season taking over, her case was closed and she was again forgotten with the passing of time, even after the accidental uncovering of her remains.

Another forgotten Australian was James Miller, whose childhood spent in institutions undoubtedly had a profound effect on the course of his life. As recorded in the Senate report, the repercussions were not only psychological and physical, but institutionalisation led many young people into antisocial and criminal behaviour, as told in this example quoted in the report – just one of many.

> In the 'outside world' I found myself completely at a loss. I was unable to behave socially and responsibly, because the rules were different but nobody had told me what they were. Before long I was in trouble with the law and, as predicted by the staff at Westbrook, found myself doing time in adult prisons. I feel that I am entitled to blame the so-called 'care givers' who, by their own actions, had shaped the innocent boy into the troubled young man who was dumped without preparation into a society that was very different to anything he had ever known.[36] (Westbrook, Sub 141).

As we have seen, Miller's police record makes for sobering reading and he ultimately died in prison in 2008, at the age of sixty-eight.

No two people are the same, nor their experiences, yet the

unanswered question will always be why some people are able to rise above their difficult childhood circumstances and make choices for a useful and fulfilling life, while others make the wrong choices and friends that lead to unproductive and unhappy lives. In this case, it all resulted in dreadful and criminal behaviour that destroyed the lives of seven girls, their families and a wider circle of affected people.

McNally Training Centre in Glen Stuart Road in Magill was a

government-run institution housed in new buildings on the site of the former Magill Reformatory, where James Miller spent much of his childhood. Boys aged between fifteen and eighteen were sent there by the juvenile court and some from remand. There were school classes, workshops in trades such as boot making and mechanics; there was a working farm and the boys were expected to learn skills to help them re-enter society. When Peter and I were visiting McNally Training Centre as volunteers in the early 70s, there were about 174 boys there. Most stayed until they were eighteen and were released under the care of a probation officer. By the time of our involvement in 1972–3, the boys had been divided into six units and a security section, which kept the 'disturbed' young men separate from the rest. The page on McNally in Find and Connect records the following assessment of the conditions at the time of our involvement:

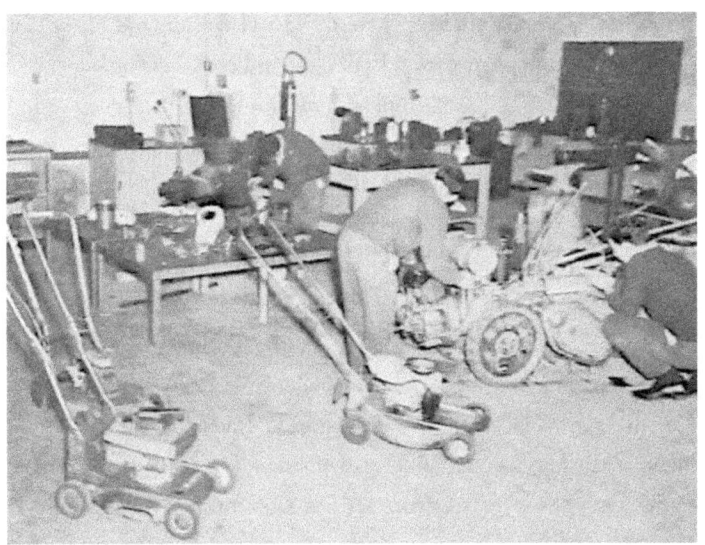

Automotive workshop at McNally Training Centre.

In 1973 a consultant psychologist who observed conditions at the McNally Training Centre for six months provided a report to the Director of the Department for Community Welfare. He described accommodation at the Centre as a series of 'locked units of incarceration'. Boys in the security section were 'locked up' under 'grossly anti-therapeutic' conditions and boys on remand were 'bewildered and bored', as well as feeling 'anxiety and apprehension due to ignorance about their fate'.[37]

Our team went in regularly on Sunday afternoons, mainly to connect with the boys, have a relaxed time with them and play some games, and to lead a brief service in the chapel. There was some security in being part of a group, but I sometimes felt nervous as the gates closed behind us and we were let into the secure buildings. It was, after all, a prison. Mostly I just felt deep compassion for these boys and young men and I knew many of them had just 'graduated' through the system of institutions until they fell foul of the law and ended up incarcerated. Undoubtedly, many of them would continue on the same trajectory and spend adult years in Yatala Prison – and meet up with many mates there.

Sometimes on our visits we felt relaxed and had good chats

with a few boys; at other times we could feel tension and knew that something had happened, and both boys and staff were on edge. The staff told us that we were the only group who took girls in there, and I think the feeling was that we had humanising effect on the residents. On reflection, I think we probably took some risks, but they were outweighed by a sense of connection with such needy young people.

When Peter graduated from college, I still had another year to finish my course. Although his family home was in Sydney and mine in Melbourne, we wanted to be near one another during our engagement, so Peter needed to find work in Adelaide while I completed my final year in Victor Harbor. Our experiences at McNally had made him interested in the rehabilitation of delinquent boys, so, as mentioned earlier, he applied to the Department for Community Welfare and was accepted into the training program as a residential care worker. After three placements, including with the younger children at Brookway Park ('heartbreaking') and Vaughan House for girls ('scary and volatile'), he subsequently chose to be placed at McNally, with on-the-job training. Working there full-time was, of course, very different from weekly voluntary visits and Peter had a roller coaster ride as he learned new skills and tried to build relationships with the boys. Sometimes he found working with the staff more challenging than with the residents. Many of his colleagues were ex-British army guardsmen and former police officers who had the young boys' welfare at heart but were pretty tough customers – perhaps necessary in such a volatile situation that could explode at any time.

It was the era when significant changes were taking place in the sector concerning exactly how to rehabilitate young offenders. Peter became a part of the new breed who were actually being trained as residential care workers, but he sometimes had doubts that the new approach was much better than the old. It was a sad reality that so many of the young men (and girls in the equivalent institution where Peter had done a placement), had only known institutions and dysfunctional or criminal families. In many cases, their time in these places had worsened their behaviour and attitudes, and some staff noted that the sort of boys who were coming through were changing from naughty boys from broken families to quite disturbed children. Peter was probably seen as rather too caring for the job – he had 70s-style long hair and the boys called him Moses – but he knew that there needed to be a relational balance to the harsher style of some of the staff.

There was one such occasion when Peter was involved in a breakout attempt at McNally, the night before we both had an important exam. One of the boys had received a message from his older brother being released from Yatala, to join him as he headed out of the state. Some boys conspired to distract Peter in the recreation room and assault the staff member with the keys so that they could escape. The incident was brought under control, though Peter was slightly injured and sent home to recover. I was very upset when I heard the news and didn't sleep well, but somehow we both fronted up to our exam the next day and passed – with Peter gaining a better result than me.

Because of Peter's shift work, our courtship was complicated, to say the least. I would travel up from Victor Harbor at the weekends, but Peter was often working when I was free. I was determined to see my fiancé but sometimes the only way was to accompany him when he took boys on outings. At this time, he was doing some shifts at the younger boys' home, Brookway Park, which had lower security, and he would drive a van full of kids for an excursion to the hills or a park. He would drop by and pick me up and we were like parents with a very large family – and counting heads every few minutes. I often baked some treats for the boys and we knew that these events were a little taste of freedom and normality for them.

One night that I will never forget, we were coming home in the dark and the boys were munching contentedly on the fudge I had made for them. Peter and I were chatting, making the most of our last few romantic minutes together in a prison van before he took the boys back to work. Suddenly I felt a little hand stroking my hair. I froze and then relaxed and just sat still. A wave of emotion flowed over me as I felt the connection with a little boy who missed his mum and just wanted to touch me. He stroked me all the way home and I didn't move or comment. That moment summed up for me how needy those kids were and, for whatever reason, what they really had lost. They were very young 'forgotten Australians' and probably set on that path for life.

Abscondings at these institutions were part of life and the news. I was highly amused when Peter and the staff took some boys to the carols night in the park, and lost most of them – the authorities were not so amused, and when it hit the press there were letters in the paper demanding harsher conditions for the inmates and raising questions about the current rehabilitation methods. As is the case today, the issue of law and order was often a political football.

After we were married in January 1974, we enjoyed three weeks' honeymoon and then it was time for Peter to return to work at McNally. As I drove him there that morning, still in the glow of our wedding and holiday, I said, somewhat flippantly, 'Imagine if all the boys had absconded. You wouldn't need to be at work.'

'In your dreams,' said Peter, 'but I can't imagine being so lucky.'

We turned on the car radio (a new luxury in our little Datsun 1200) only to hear the headline:

> Nine boys escaped from McNally Training Centre last night and are still at large. There have been calls for better security at this institution.

We laughed very loudly in disbelief and kept driving. At least Peter's return to work would be a gentle one – maybe. Our working life as a married couple had begun.

In the following year, plans were drawn up for a new section of McNally to be established in the suburbs as a kind of halfway house for boys ready to be released. This unit would prepare them for their return to life outside and would operate more like a family unit with minimum security. Peter was chosen to be on the team establishing this unit, which, to our amazement, was to be in Glandore, just around the corner from our home in Everard Park. We weighed the offer up, because the round-the-clock shifts would include nights, and I actually felt a little uncomfortable having the place so close to our home. Peter accepted the appointment, mainly because it would be so much more satisfying to work with the boys towards re-entry and also because the short trip to work was going to save so much travel time. It was a good decision, because he loved going out to industries and finding work for the boys, although I didn't enjoy the strong smell of roll-your-own Drum tobacco that pervaded his clothes and hair every shift and I insisted that he shower before he kissed me.

This background with the Department for Community Welfare was the context for our involvement with Veronica; we understood a little of institutional life that she had come from. I still find it strange that we did not ask her much about her childhood. Maybe we were living life in the fast lane and took her along with us for those years, and did not look back.

I have pored over her album, trying to find clues to track down her history, but with little success. Minda Home is the only recognisable institution and we were to find out later on that her grave was paid for by Minda and is in the 'Minda section' of the cemetery. From birth to death, she was a Minda girl.

14

1980: A Verdict

'On the count of murder of Veronica Knight: not guilty.' The foreman of the jury paused, then read out six counts of 'guilty' for the murder of each of the other girls: Sylvia Pittman, Juliet Mykyta, Vicki Howell, Connie Iordanides, Tania Kenny and Deborah Lamb.

Justice Matheson immediately sentenced Miller to six life sentences. Two sobbing women were led out from the court.

Miller, silent until now, leaned over the dock and yelled, 'You filthy liar, Lawrie – you mongrel!'

One of his sisters joined in from the front row and screamed at Detectives Lawrie and Foster. The eight-hour wait for the long anticipated verdict was over.

It was 9.18 p.m. on 11 March 1980 when the jury returned for the last time. The trial had been going since 12 February, which was exactly three years to the day from the last death in 1977. Preceded by a committal hearing in the magistrates' court before Mr W.R. Harniman the previous September, this dramatic trial in the Supreme Court had mesmerised the city of Adelaide for a full month. The newspapers gave detailed accounts of the case daily, often accompanied by Viktor Bohdan's evocative sketches of the scenes in court.

The jury of six men and six women had been called to listen to the evidence in the most sensational murder case in South Australian history and they had finally reached their decision. If I had been there in court, I probably would not have heard any more after the 'not guilty' for Veronica. Over three years after her death, no one was to be made legally

Anne-Marie Mykyta, mother of Truro victim Julie Mykyta, listening to evidence.

accountable for the tragic loss of her life. Christopher Worrell was dead and James Miller, a career criminal who spent his fortieth birthday, like most of his birthdays, in prison waiting for a verdict, won his argument that he could not have known that Worrell would kill her. Many years later, the absence of a conviction still grieves me.

The trial had opened with Miller in the dock, accompanied by one police officer. The press were represented by Bob Whitington and Peter De Ionno, who had written extensively for the papers about the case as it progressed. Mr B.J. Jennings was the Crown Prosecutor, and Mr K.P. Duggans QC handled Miller's defence. The trial stalled in technicalities for some time at the start as the issue of the legality of the police evidence was examined. Their sixteen hours of interviews with Miller were the basis of their case, but there was little if any scientific evidence to back it up so its acceptance in court was critical to the prosecution's case.

The police decision to take Miller out to the burial sites on the night he was arrested to retrieve the last three bodies before he could speak to a solicitor was controversial; the decision had been taken in the confidence that the court would uphold it as a reasonable thing to do, given the nature of the crimes and the overriding need for the families to know where their daughters' remains were. Obviously, a solicitor's advice to his client would be to remain silent, and the rest of the bodies might never have been found. It was risky to interrogate him before he was formally charged, but fortunately the evidence was admitted and the trial progressed on Wednesday 20 February. There has always been disagreement between the police record which stated that he never requested legal support, and Miller's claims that he asked for a solicitor and was denied.

Police evidence was presented first by the Crown Prosecutor, Jennings, with Detective Glen Lawrie of the Major Crime Squad as the chief witness. The sordid story as told by Miller to the police in his confession after the night trip to Truro was read out, word by horrifying word. The families had to listen to the distressing details, and yet they craved the truth. Even at this point it was denied to them, as we now know that much of what Miller said to the police was not true. He lied then, and probably lied in his account in his book, and it will never be clear which parts of his statements were true. There were to be important differences between the police interview records and his later, unsworn statement in court. My hope is that the latter version is nearer the truth – that Veronica's life ended in Greenhill Road somewhere in the hills and that she was not alive during the long drive to Truro.

June Sylvia Tait, Veronica's nurse friend from Minda days, testified, as did William Richard Thomas, who stumbled on her remains and went back to check with his wife, Valda. The court also heard that Lawrie had asked Miller why he had assisted Worrell, to which he replied, 'I don't know…we'd picked up girls before and nothing happened.'

Lawrie then asked the question that we all would ask, 'Why didn't you try and stop Chris?'

'I couldn't do much without endangering myself, and I really believe that.'[38]

The families were called to give evidence again as they had in the

committal hearing, describing in agonising detail their daughters' movements and when they were last seen; one parent – generally the mother – would be in the dock while the other supported from the body of the courtroom. Their anguish was palpable as each was forced to tell the tragic stories yet again. The papers had photos of the parents leaving court after their testimony and, for forty years, I thought, 'There was no one there for Veronica.'

The hiding of the bodies was discussed next on Friday 22 March by Constable First Class Ian Congdon of the police technical services, who was involved in the recovery of all the bodies. Photos of the sites were shown to the jury to prepare them for their trip to view the area. Testimony was heard from the car dealer who lent Worrell and Miller the infamous white Valiant as a replacement car, which ultimately led to Worrell's death in the crash. Court was then adjourned until the following week.

On Tuesday 26 February, the murder trial took a dramatic excursion out of the courtroom to inspect the sites where the remains were found – Swamp Road, Truro, Port Gawler and Wingfield. The jurors and legal teams travelled in air-conditioned Mercedes, with Miller handcuffed to his police companions in the following vehicle.

The press were held back from the immediate area, but managed to take photos that dominated the media the next day and have become some of the iconic images of the event.

Now it was time to call the key witness whose information had led the police to Miller. Although her name was suppressed at the time, Amelia was next in the crown's case. She told of Worrell and Miller's close friendship and that Miller had told her after the funeral what Worrell had done. She defended the fact that she had not gone to the police because she felt that they were looking for a scapegoat and that she did not believe him. Her evidence, however, was vague; full of 'maybe', 'can't recall' and 'possibly'. Miller glared at her and later alleged that she had been coached. Her story in court was very different to Miller's account in his book. She quoted Miller as saying that the girls 'were just rags', a comment that he later denied.

There was little forensic evidence to bring to court, but Dr C.H. Manock, director of forensic pathology at the Institute of Medical and Veterinary Science, testified that he had examined all the remains. In the absence of other wounds from shooting, stabbing or beating, he assumed that the cause of death in all cases was strangulation, but this could not be demonstrated categorically so long after the time of death.

The crown closed its case and there would be no witnesses for the defence. To a hushed court, it was announced that Miller would read an unsworn statement to the court, which would effectively protect him from cross-examination under oath. Then there was a rustle of anticipation as the full court prepared to hear from the accused for the first time on the following Monday 10 March. What *would* he say? What *could* he say?

The public gallery of Court 2 was full, with fifty people seated by 11.15 a.m. It was guarded by heavy security and people were turned away as the public pressed in to hear the accused killer speak. The history of an unsworn statement, sometimes known as a 'dock statement', has its origins in the fear that a defendant charged with murder might perjure himself, and thus risk his soul by making untrue statements under oath. Therefore, an accused murderer was given the privilege of addressing the court without swearing on the Bible and without being required to answer any questions. The practice was abolished in some states, including South Australia in 1985, although there is a case still made nationally for indigenous defendants requiring this privilege as they may have difficulty under cross-examination.[39] Many feel that when the practice was still in use, it gave a psychological advantage to the defendant, who could speak more freely and naturally and possibly sway the jury towards believing his innocence. Given Miller's lack of education, many believe that he received a great deal of coaching and assistance with his statement.

Miller began immediately to read his fifty-page statement, which took him fifty minutes to finish. Beginning with his background, he told the assembled crowd that his parents were alive and that his family consisted of four sisters and a brother, and that he had almost no education due to a life in prison. He claimed that he and Worrell frequently picked up girls and drove to isolated spots and that nothing untoward had happened before Veronica's death.

He recounted that they had offered Veronica a ride from King William Street, as she needed to get home to her hostel. Instead, they drove up Greenhill Road and turned up a sidetrack. He said that he went for a walk and that Worrell killed Veronica while he was gone. His story now was that Worrell was in a dark mood and threatened him with a knife and that, as a result, he drove as directed to Truro. The next day they returned to work at the Unley Council as if all were normal. Miller did not report the death to the police because he did not want to lose the only friend he had.

The macabre story continued. On 6 January 1977, they picked up Tania Kenny in a borrowed car, a Holden this time. They went to a house to pick up clothes for Miller, and Tania died there. Miller objected that he did not want the location to be connected with the murder, so they drove to Wingfield, where she was buried in a shallow grave. He claimed that they drove around in a predatory fashion every night picking up girls – at least thirty or forty apart from the Truro victims.

Julie Mykyta was picked up on 21 January, driven to Angle Vale and assaulted. Miller was aware of Worrell's murderous intent and walked away twice, leaving Julie to her fate.

Sylvia Pittman was picked up at the railway station on Sunday 6 February and taken to Grand Junction Road. When Miller returned from his walk, she was dead.

The next day, Monday 7 February, Vicki Howell was taken from near the post office to the hills at the end of Unley Road and, once again, Miller went away twice, leaving Worrell to his crime. Each time, he drove the car to dispose of the bodies.

Two days later, on Wednesday 9 February, Connie Iordanides was given a ride at 9 p.m. from King William Street. Miller apparently again went away twice, allowing Worrell time to take his next victim.

Finally, on Saturday 12 February, Deborah Lamb accepted a ride in Hindley Street and was taken to Port Gawler. Miller, who must have known what would follow, went for another walk, and another life was taken. Each girl was sexually assaulted and strangled. Miller dispassionately chronicled the horrific story to a silent court.

There were some differences in his story from what he told the police in his interview, most notably regarding the locations of the murders, which he admitted to lying about. He now said that none of the girls had died at Truro, but five bodies had been taken there. He concluded with the claim

> I was just the chauffeur and the mug… Irrespective of my weakness in my behaviour and my attachment to Worrell, I am not a murderer and I did not plan or in any way help to murder any of these girls… I now know that remaining silent after Worrell killed the first girl has cost the lives of six other girls.[40]

Court was adjourned in preparation for the summing up to follow the next day.

I can make no judgement on the veracity of any of Miller's story. His unsworn statement is closer to his account in his book than the police interview, but both contain anomalies, and he does comment that because there were so many girls, much of his detail came from what he read or saw in the media. It is included here for completeness of the account of the trial. There is no way of verifying the testimony of a lifelong criminal who was a compulsive liar, particularly when he was facing a conviction that would put him away for the rest of his life and was well aware that no one remained to contradict him. He told crime writer Nigel Hunt that he and Worrell had formed a pact that there would be no survivors to identify them.[41] For Anne-Marie Mykyta, who was not able to get into the crowded court that day, the statement emphasised for her that the victims could not defend themselves in the same way.

The penultimate day of the trial commenced with the Crown summing up. Mr Jennings, in his three-hour speech, reflected my sentiments now when he told the court that they would never know the truth, but should be quite clear that it was a 'horrible truth'. He asserted that in the joint criminal enterprise, both Miller and Worrell had every reason not to risk being recognised by their victims. They would have pointed their fingers at both the man who had sexually assaulted them and the man who ignored their plight and drove them to their deaths. Jennings presented the version that the girls were killed at Truro and that Miller had minimised his part and, at the very least, was a voyeur to the crimes.

Mr Duggan, for the defence, spoke to the jury and warned them against looking for a scapegoat as they looked at Miller in the dock. They were reminded that driving the car and even disposing of bodies was not what he was charged with – they had to prove that murder was his intent, not just an event at which he was present and witnessed. He argued that Miller was 'trapped in a web of circumstance'. He cast aspersions on Amelia's evidence and went so far as to say that she had actually assisted the defence. His address was completed the next morning, on what would be the last day of a dramatic trial that had drawn unprecedented attention.

Justice Matheson then summed up the case and warned the jury about the effect of their emotions on their decision – which was immediately illustrated by an emotional outburst by a young woman in the gallery who was then escorted from the court. He went back over the events of the case, giving a chronological account of each crime. When referring to the inconsistencies between the police record of interview and Miller's version in his unsworn statement, Matheson pointed out that the police had given their evidence under oath, while the accused chose not to swear to the truth of his account, resulting in his immunity to cross-examination. The jury retired just before 1 p.m.

After dealing with a question during the afternoon, Justice Matheson said he would not take a verdict before 7.15 p.m. At 7.50 p.m., the jury returned to a full and hushed court, but had only reached unanimity on the first and third counts – the murders of Veronica and Julie. They retired again, only to return yet again at about 9 p.m., requesting further clarification on the term 'joint enterprise'. After Matheson had discussed with the legal teams how it could be explained, he said,

> If you are satisfied beyond reasonable doubt that the accused and Worrell were acting in concert to pick up a girl, and that the accused drove Worrell and that girl to Truro or somewhere else and it was within the contemplation of Miller that that particular girl may be murdered, then he is guilty of murder.[42]

This clarification brought an immediate outcome and eight minutes later the jury were back. They had made their decisions: not guilty for Veronica's death, guilty for the other six girls. The use of the word 'may' in the explanation, as distinct from 'would' in an earlier presentation, was to become a moot point in later discussion, and even the basis of a call for a mistrial. It sealed Miller's fate, because at least for the six girls after Veronica, he must have known that they might be killed. I would contend that, at the very least, he probably also knew what would happen to Veronica. His involvement was almost certainly much deeper than he ever admitted.

The sentencing followed immediately – six life sentences. Miller went back to Yatala to begin his incarceration, and claimed later in his book that he had indeed been made a scapegoat and convicted for someone else's crimes. But for the Truro murders, it was established legally that there were two perpetrators: one dead and one incarcerated for life.

15

1980: An Editorial

The murder trial was finally over and the people of Adelaide could look forward to reading news of different events on the front pages of the newspapers. *The Advertiser*, presumably in an attempt to summarise all that had just transpired, published an editorial on Friday 14 March 1980 that stunned the families of the victims. Anne-Marie Mykyta, mother of Julie, could not believe the words that she read, and reproduced the key part of the editorial in her book from memory – it was seared on her brain.

The newspaper, a pioneer of sensational headlines from the 1950s, set out to draw some lessons from an event that had affected the whole community. The editor referred to Worrell as a 'monster' and 'depraved creature' and, oddly, made no mention of Miller, who had just been convicted of six murders, contending that there would be more of these dangerous people with the advent of the permissive age. There was only one solution, according to the editor:

> It is clearly the duty of the parents of girls, particularly the naïve, the gullible and the misguidedly adventurous, to impress upon them the dangers of walking alone in the streets at night and accepting lifts in cars offered by people unknown to them… Girls who tend to be free with their favours are committing no offence by behaving as they choose, but they must realise that in doing so they are exposing themselves to mortal danger.[43]

I read this and join Anne-Marie Mykyta's shock and dismay in response; from today's #MeToo awareness in our culture, these words come across as victim-blaming and insensitive. These were girls going about their own business, mostly looking for public transport to get home. There is no evidence for this collective portrayal of them as 'loose' women; at worst, they each made a bad decision to accept a lift with two men who could have been father and son. The only evidence of them being 'free with their favours' is Miller's unsworn story. We will never know the degree of coercion, but these men were, put simply, predators, and still the girls were being judged to be partly responsible for their fate.

From the outset, even the police made assumptions about the lifestyles of these teenagers, brushing aside the protestations of families and friends, who knew that something bad had happened from the time of their disappearance. We knew that Veronica would not have missed her trip to visit us; the matron of her hostel went to the police within two hours of her disappearance because Veronica had never missed curfew, and never failed to communicate her whereabouts. Her friends at St Bartholomew's Anglican Church were extremely worried about her and wondered what was being done to find her. Retired detective Len Brown (who turned a hundred in 2017), a member of that church, lent his assistance and made enquiries about the case.

> Families of missing persons, if they want action, often have to continually justify to the police, the press and the community that the missing person has not simply run away. In many cases, the police assume the person has run away until it is proven that there may be evidence of foul play. Clearly there were problems with the police investigation from the start.[44]

One of the reasons for writing this book is to dispel the widely held perception that these seven girls were somehow to blame for their deaths. This compounded the frustration and anguish for the parents and families at the time, and has persisted until now in the memories of the event that were shaped by media articles like this one. The victims were robbed not only of their lives, but of their reputations as well. For those who lost their daughters and family members, a slur remains forever.

Veronica's life has been largely forgotten by many as the years passed, but the few memories that remain are tainted by articles such as these, books that base themselves on pseudo facts, and true crime websites and podcasts that continue to reproduce errors and are selectively highlighting sensational aspects of the cases they broadcast. Those who editorialise on these events without acknowledging the facts must take some responsibility for attitudes that persist until the present. Females are still portrayed as being, to some degree, guilty when predators harm them – for simply being on the street and at the bus stop. There is a sense in which this story is my reply to this editorial and these sites.

16

2017: A Plan

'I need to go to Adelaide, Peter,' I said one morning. 'I know we're saving to travel next year, but I can do it cheaply. I'll drive over and stay in an Airbnb. I just need to go there and be where Veronica was, find out more about her life and see if I can find anyone to speak to.'

Peter didn't want me to have to go on my own, but I knew he was busy and to take a week out would put his projects on hold. I considered that this book was my project, so I dropped the discussion and started looking at the diary in the weeks ahead, researched cheap air fares and car rental, compared that with driving and the time and energy it would take. I blocked in a week towards the end of October and wrote 'Trip to Adelaide' in the calendar, fitting it in between all sorts of commitments and events. Then I let it settle to see how I felt about it. I like to plan but I also need to 'feel' the plan and know it is right. This felt more and more right and in my mind, I knew I needed to go. I am a person often driven by my head and needing to listen more often to my heart.

A list began to grow: the hostels, Rundle Mall and King William Street, Veronica's grave, Brian and Ruth, and…Truro. That was when it hit me – could I really go to Truro on my own? I had found a very inexpensive bungalow to stay in and it would cost no more for Peter to come with me and stay there if we drove. We talked some more and he insisted that he always intended to come and that we would have a little holiday as well. So it was settled and I booked the accommodation and began to wonder who I could find who would still be alive and able to remember anything. This would be a challenge; forty years is a long time. Even we ourselves are very much senior citizens. My hope was that some things must be hard to forget.

Sleuthing had become a habit for me. I scoured newspaper articles, made lists of names, hunted in the white pages and cross-referenced information. I sent out a few tentative letters, wondering if I would ever receive any replies. A couple of names were distinctive and I felt sure I had the right people: Ken Thorsen was the retired police commander who headed the case. Would he be prepared to speak to me? Charles Cornwall was Worrell's parole officer and he had written his memoirs, which I found online and sourced. Would he respond, let alone be willing to see me? I felt sure that they had had their share of people looking for sensational stories over the years, and I spent a long time composing my letters with enough information to convince them of my worthy motives but not so much that they would throw the letter in the bin. I did, indeed, feel as if I was 'casting my bread upon the waters', but I had nothing to lose and everything to gain. My mission was gaining momentum.

I had already read all the books and all the newspaper articles I could find, and had developed a detailed timeline to which I added more and more confirmed facts and dates. I had woven into it our own significant dates and times, and was startled to realise that the dreadful events in Adelaide were unfolding just as we left the country to go overseas. Why is it so shocking to align events with one's own personal actions? Why does it make a difference to know exactly what we were doing when a tragic event happened? Would anything have changed if I had been doing something else? Of course not. Was I in some way negligent not to know about it? Again, of course not. Perhaps there is a little element of survivor guilt in there somewhere – and we have always struggled with the thought that had Veronica not been preparing to visit us, she might not have been in the city that night. Our episodic memory is very strong, even in people who are losing their memories, and somehow to know exactly where I was and what

I was doing at that time just highlighted for me that terrible things can happen while we are getting on with our lives. I imagine that if we knew all the horror being perpetrated just while we eat our dinner or weed the garden, we could not bear it and were not meant to.

In spite of all this, I was determined to return to the place where the events took place, and, no matter how painful it would turn out to be, my intention was to put myself in Veronica's forgotten shoes for a short while. I had no idea what a profound pilgrimage I was setting out to experience. I certainly underestimated the effect it would have on others, all of us co-victims of this terrible event that took place forty long years ago. In addition, I had temporarily forgotten that while this was my book project, Veronica was our girl. Peter and I needed, of course, to do this together…

17

October 2017: A Reply

As the weeks went by, I prepared as much as I could for our trip. I sent a list of questions to Brian and Ruth, now in their eighties, who did their best to answer them for me. I felt the sensitivity of raising such painful memories so long after the event and was not surprised when they found it hard to remember details. Brian barely remembers the funeral he took for Veronica – understandably in the light of how many funerals he would have conducted over a lifetime of service – but he kindly tracked down the record for me, now stored at another church. As a couple who have given so much hospitality to others, they struggle to recall that Veronica lived with them for a month, although their children remember her being there. We have all moved on with our lives over the forty years since these events happened and memories inevitably decay and fade.

I tracked down the diocesan archivist of the Anglican Church in Adelaide and managed to obtain the documentation and date for our confirmation together in the cathedral. Veronica's grave is registered online and I was able to request a photo of the headstone. I gazed at it for a long time, as if somehow looking at the picture made it even more real. As part of that search, I discovered the location of Worrell's grave as well and set it aside without much thought. This was to be about Veronica, I told myself, not the perpetrator, who has already had enough attention.

My quest to find her personal information was not very successful. I wrote to Find and Connect pleading for the right to know about

Veronica's life and details, but to no avail. Without being a relative, I did not expect to break through the wall of privacy and, despite my good intentions, I understood entirely, but was disappointed. How could I give a voice to this girl if I cannot find out anything about most of her life?

I pored over maps – located hostels, cemeteries, shopping arcades, searched for photo booths (do they still exist?) and institutions and started to plan what to do in the week in Adelaide. How would the breakthrough come? How could I connect? Repeatedly I looked up Swamp Road near Truro on digital maps and stared at the pattern of the trees and scrub until I had almost memorised the shapes of the clumps of bush. How would I know where they found her? Would anyone remember, and what were the chances of finding people from so long ago? Very slim.

There were blurry photos in Mykyta's and Miller's books, but none really definitive. A sketch map in a newspaper article was clearly not to scale, but at least had the names of the roads on it. Halfway House Road. Swamp Road. Sandleton Road. Did it matter what the name of the road was if you were already dead? Why did the two men go back to that area five times? That seemed a foolish way to cover tracks – but what would I know about the psychology of a psychopathic killer? I felt as if I were in a very alien country with no name. Would there be fences too hard to get through? Were there fences back then? Who owns the land? Did the other girls' families go out there to Truro to see where their daughters were found? Would it all be just too dark and scary?

My book had become a beast that was constantly filling my thoughts with unanswerable questions and I began to wonder why I had unleashed it when there were so many gentler topics that I could have tackled. Did I really expect to be able to answer even a few of the questions that were lining up for my attention, pushing and shoving like a year eight class outside one of my classrooms when I was a teacher. My life had to go on – the garden was demanding attention as it does in spring, grandchildren needed to be minded and dropped off to swimming training, meals always to be planned and cooked, my patient husband trying not to interrupt me when I sat at my writing desk with books and newspaper articles spread everywhere.

I had to keep my desk tidy so that my grandchildren would not see 'Tandem Killers', 'Horror in the Truro Scrub' or 'Seven girls missing: serial killer' where Grandma sits. It became a discipline not to zone out and go into my private world of disturbing questions when an event became boring, a TV show less than engaging or a sermon too long.

Friends who had enjoyed reading my autobiography would ask what I was writing now, and I had to find a way of answering while avoiding long explanations containing murder and mayhem. They might get worried about me. 'Just researching and writing about a young friend of mine…' I would say in as offhand a way as I could, hoping there would be no probing questions.

Occasionally when people probed, I could not help myself and tried to explain the story, but discovered there was only the very short version or a very long version and not much in between. I resolved to talk only to a couple of good friends so that I would feel that I had a semblance of control over this bizarre adventure that had somehow overtaken me. In the back of my mind, however, was the confronting thought that the book would be put out there for people to read in the end and there would be no hiding then. I am sure my grandchildren will want to read it and that knowledge has guided some of my decisions in the way I have written.

Podcasts became my new addiction: *Cold Case Files, Trace Evidence, Australian True Crime* and *Trace*. Anything to do with missing girls, murder, solving cases, forensic science, discovery of bodies, people who disappeared off the street – I listened while I was driving, gardening or walking and gleaned information about cases and procedures, effects on families and clues that broke open cases. I had joined a world of crime junkies and I felt a little guilty to be such a voyeur but also strangely exhilarated by all that I was learning. At times I identified too much with the families left without resolution, and other times with those who found the truth as we did, and lived with the terrible facts. I realised that the world is a seriously troubled place for many and something in me began to stir as it slowly dawned on me that Peter and I were co-victims in this case, along with a large circle of others affected as well. It was as if I had taken a mighty leap into the air and came back to earth in a foreign and unsettling landscape.

Then it arrived. A handwritten envelope addressed to me containing a letter written on A4 paper – it was an answer to my carefully worded letter sent a week or more before to Ken Thorsen. The date at the top of the letter was Friday 22 September 2017. Yes, he would be happy to speak to me. Suddenly I wished I was heading to Adelaide immediately rather than in two weeks' time and I became aware of my heart thumping, slightly out of its rhythm, as is its wont. Now I had somewhere to take my questions. I read the letter again: 'You have located the person you are looking for.' That was police-speak, using 'located' instead of 'found'. He had documents and records to show me and…the Report of Missing Person. My heart nearly bumped out of my chest as I took in the import of that. That would reveal information we had longed to know, I was sure.

I set the letter aside to calm myself and wondered when would be the best time to phone him. The next day was Saturday – but it was the grand final and the South Australian Crows were playing – perhaps better to wait. Nevertheless, I was extremely impatient to make contact and to set up an appointment during the week we would be in Adelaide. After forty years of letting this beast lie low and hibernate, it was waking up and a sense of urgency took over.

The road trip to Adelaide would be much more significant than I ever imagined.

18

2017: A Connection

'Hello. Is that Mr Ken Thorsen?' I ask when the phone is answered by a strong male voice. 'This is Jeanette Woods from Melbourne. I wrote to you about…'

'I know who you are,' he cuts in. 'I am happy to talk to you.'

I hardly know where to begin. At last, I have managed to make direct contact with someone who was involved in Veronica's case nearly forty years ago. It is such a long time ago, and key figures back in the 70s have not only retired, but many have died – like Mrs Anne-Marie Mykyta and her husband, Irush. Dick Wordley, the well-known journalist who helped James Miller write his account of the events, has also died. Others may still be alive, but are in their eighties and even their nineties.

Ken Thorsen sounds clear and strong. He later tells me that he is eighty-eight, but he sounds much younger. I explain a little of my motivation in writing about Veronica.

'She was the first…to…go, wasn't she?' he asks. 'And she was found over a year later by mushroom hunters?'

'That's right,' I reply. 'It was on Anzac Day in 1978, nearly sixteen months later.'

We chat a little and I am astounded by his clear memory and ascertain that he would be happy for me to visit him in Adelaide. Amazingly, Ken has copies stored at home of the missing person's report and the interviews with James Miller, and will make them available to me when I visit. I can hardly believe that this window has opened up.

Although I will see him in a couple of weeks' time, I ask a few critical questions that simply can't wait. 'May I ask you if you think that James Miller was guilty of more than being the driver and bystander for the murders?' I tentatively enquire.

'Of course he was!' comes the adamant reply. Ken says he had a great deal to do with Miller over the years and saw him often in prison. His considered opinion is that Miller was protecting himself and was a 'bad piece of work'. He tells me Miller was not popular in prison and was generally self-serving.

My next question is an important one. 'Did you go to the place in Truro where the bodies were found?'

'Of course,' he replies.

I ask him if he could pinpoint on a map for me exactly where the remains were found so that I might be able to visit the spot, and he assures me that he could, and that he has a very clear map.

We make arrangements for my visit, and then talk a little more. Somehow, it feels reassuring to hear his steady voice and I feel somehow that I have made a first connection with Veronica and that period of time so long ago. I also feel elated that my research skills had succeeded and that speaking with Commander Thorsen is a great breakthrough for me. Ken tells me that he does not use a mobile phone so that he is not harassed. That is a sobering reminder to me that his long career has not been without cost. I can't wait to meet him.

For my part, I end the conversation by telling him that Veronica was a lovely girl, not 'loose' or rebellious. I tell him that she attended church regularly with us and stayed in our home, and was always helpful and loving, if a bit cheeky. I tell him that we always knew that something bad had happened to her and that she did not run away or hitchhike to Melbourne without telling anyone – especially us. After forty years, I am finally able to speak in her defence to someone who was significantly involved in the case. On reflection, I realise that while she will never come back, I have at last taken a huge step in my quest to honour her memory. There was much more to come.

19

2017: A Trip

On Sunday 22 October 2017, we pack our cases, fill the car and lock up the house. It has been at least three years since we drove from Melbourne to Adelaide but we know the trip well. The distance between the small towns gets further and further and the green turns to brown as the road heads north-west towards South Australia. We share the driving, stretching at each changeover. Coffee at Gong Gong, sandwiches at Bungalally Green Lake, snacks at Bordertown and then the push across the Murray flood plain and finally the long downhill freeway through the hills to Adelaide.

We have visited the beautiful city of Adelaide many times since we left in 1976, but have never before done what we intend to do on this trip, although I am not sure why. Our plan is to retrace, as far as possible, Veronica's last days, her important locations, the hostels where she lived and the places where we spent time with her. We have meetings arranged with significant people in her story and, nearly forty years after she was buried, we will visit her grave for the first time, and make the difficult journey – Anne-Marie Mykyta's 'Long Way' to Truro. I look at the city with fresh eyes. What will we discover in this week?

We sleep well after our big drive and head out early on Monday morning, eager to use our time well. Our first stop is a quick and nostalgic visit to the house in Myrtlebank where Peter boarded during our engagement year in 1973. So many happy memories. Now forty-four years have passed; we are parents and grandparents of a clan of

seventeen and have travelled all over the world. In contrast, our young friend from those days barely reached adulthood before her life ended.

The road works, detours and one-way streets surrounding the CBD bamboozle us as we try to find a way into a central car park so that we can explore the city block on foot. In our day, Rundle Street was open to traffic, but in September 1976, soon after we left, it was closed off at King William Street and Pulteney Street. Premier Don Dunstan unveiled the street as one of the first pedestrian malls in Australia, complete with cobbled brickworks and shady trees. Only weeks later, with its late opening hours, it became a novel and inviting place for Adelaide residents to browse and enjoy Christmas shopping. Suddenly I feel overwhelmed as I try to imagine where Veronica would have walked as she and her friend enjoyed the atmosphere of the Mall.

We begin to wander the arcades, wondering if there are any photo booths still in use. The sun is shining, buskers are out in force and the iconic silver ball installation reflects back our distorted figures. Our kids loved it when we brought them in to see Santa in 1980, completely unaware that James Miller's committal trial and the Supreme Court trial had taken place earlier that year. I sit in the warm sun and search on my iPad for clues that might help us. Peter speaks to a jeweller in an arcade who remembers the events of Truro and says that he grew up where one of the killers had lived. It seems that everyone in Adelaide has a link somehow. Whomever we speak to knows someone related to one of the families, or lives near someone connected to the case.

I find a website that mentions photo booths at the Myer Centre, which has now been completely rebuilt. Feeling as though we might find the booths, we are again deflated when the woman in the information booth says that the black-and-white ones were taken away about three years ago. It seems that they are rented out these days for parties and occasions, so they are moved around to many locations. We stand near the lift well and take photographs where they used to be located, wondering if we are in the right spot.

Time passes as we wander, eat and window-shop, imagining two young girls shopping for clothes and gifts. Which shops attracted them? What was the dress she bought like? Did she have presents for us that we never received? There must have been a large amount of cash in her purse before her purchases, as there was $180 left when the men emptied her purse and threw it away.

I am feeling tired, not just physically, and we are feeling our emotional reserves draining as we step out this little pilgrimage. Now it is time to take the 450-metre walk to the bus stop in King William Street at the western end of the mall. We walk past all the bus stops for the various routes; today we would need to take bus 99 to go to Angas Street East. Which number bus did she need to catch?

I feel tense as we walk towards 100 King William Street, the site of the old Majestic Hotel. It is as if I am literally walking in Veronica's footsteps. There it is: number 100, now a group of shops. Right in front is a loading zone, a single-vehicle space in front of all the bus terminals that is the only spot for a car to pull up briefly. Peter takes photos, feeling as though he is forty years too late in documenting the scene of the crime. For the first time, I feel a wave of emotion as I picture the scenario that I have read about so many times and have been pondering over these last months. Getting into the car right here was the last decision she made, and it was a bad one. I actually shiver.

Peter retrieves our car from the parking centre and returns to pull up in that very same spot at 100 King William Street. I get in with him and we drive off, silent with our own thoughts. That's all it takes to drive away in a car. Forever.

We are on our way to the first interview – with Ken Thorsen. This feels momentous, and it is. Ken and his wife, Betty, meet us at the door of their neat unit in the senior residents' village. Their impeccable

home looks out over the back to a golf course and is in a peaceful and desirable corner of the village. We sit down while Betty offers drinks, and size each other up. Ken is eighty-eight and they have been married an impressive sixty-nine years. I feel grateful again that I have found him while he still remembers so much so clearly and is willing to talk to me. I am not very experienced at this kind of interview but know that I need to establish at the start that I may take notes of our conversation and may also quote him in the book. Ken is generous with his permission. He tells me that he will be a guest speaker on the Truro events at a function next week, so talking to me today is good preparation. I take from this that Truro is still a live topic in Adelaide.

Ken shows me his videos, and shares cuttings and other documents while Peter goes to work photographing all that he can. We munch on Betty's delicious egg sandwiches while I allow Ken to go at his own speed.

Betty gently suggests we sit up at the table but Ken says firmly, 'No, we'll stay here.' The ex-commander has this event under control.

So we stay where we are on the sofas and I try to work through the list of questions I had prepared, but Ken will take this at his own pace, I suspect. Then he hands over the document I had been waiting for – the Report of Missing Person. I don't ask why or how he still has it, but I'm glad he does and cannot believe that after all this time we will hold the piece of paper and know exactly what was reported on the fateful night.

My eyes flick straight to the line that says, 'Missing person was supposed to go to Melbourne on Sunday to 190 The Avenue PARKVILLE VIC… her train ticket is still back at the Salvation Army

Hostel.' That's us. That's our address in typewritten letters on a police document. Steadily I feel as though we are, after all these years, re-establishing our connection with our girl, not just in our hearts, but officially. I think it is that sort of moment for Ken too. He is looking at us – the people noted on his own police document. No police contacted us in 1976, but we are here now, sitting in the living room of the senior police officer responsible at that time. What's a wait of forty years? I also note that the report says that she returned to City Cross Arcade – if only we had known that this morning. That's where the photo booths were.

Next, Ken gives us James Miller's police record sheets – pages and pages of them. The word 'larceny' appears repeatedly, with 'shop-breaking' and 'car-breaking' becoming more frequent as he gets older. I glance at the record and confirm what I already know – he was first sent to the Magill Reformatory as an eleven-year-old. Meanwhile, Peter is reading the record of the police interviews with Miller the night he was arrested. We are permitted only to photograph the section about Veronica. It is very confronting, as we knew it would be. Sitting quietly for a while, we both scan the pages. Ken gives us some time; he knows this is difficult for us to read. There is also new information about Miller's original name – Melville Raymond Just. I note that I have seen 'Melvyn' in other sources, like Miller's own book, and think that his own version of his original name is more likely to be true (unlike some other things he said in his book).

I begin to describe Veronica a little and our history with her, but can see that Ken does not connect strongly with what I am saying. I was to understand later, on reflection, that Ken's perspective was a police view and he remembers it all as a 'case'. There were, after all, seven victims, of whom Veronica was just one. He even says that it did not matter that there was no conviction for Veronica, as they only needed one or more 'guilty' to get Miller into prison for life. But to us it does matter.

He talks at length about the Major Crime Investigation Unit that he was asked to form and lead, taking its shape from Scotland Yard, and how that made a difference to the Truro case, as compared to the 'fiasco' of the Beaumont case. Ken was awarded an Order of Australia for his work, as was his deputy. He has regrets to this day that the two detectives who did most of the legwork were never recognised. One was Bob Giles, who cracked the pattern of killings and brought it to his attention. Ken has continued to try and, as recently as last year, had an article written by the crime journalist for *The Advertiser*, Nigel Hunt, drawing attention once again to their work and asking for awards for his men. From my perspective, I agree that Sergeant Bob Giles should be honoured for his work in this case.

I think he is proud of the way the case was handled, which is a different perspective from ours until now, and sees it as a step up in investigative policing. They did, after all, find the perpetrator and get convictions, as well as locating the bodies. I need to absorb what I am hearing today and adjust my views on the way the case was managed. I mentally asterisk this issue for further thought.

The other positive outcome from the case was an eventual change in the law. It is common knowledge now that the police actually broke the law and their own procedural guidelines when they took Miller out in the middle of the night and located the body of Julie Mykyta. When a suspect was arrested, he was supposed to be taken immediately to the nearest police station, and either charged or bailed. Out of compassion for the family, however, they broke the law, but they did the thing that was right. Years later, they were able to get the law changed so that now the police have four hours to question a suspect, and can ask for another four hours if needed. As Ken explains this to us, I understand that he considers this one of his important achievements. I am also beginning to comprehend how he frames the case and I feel even more determined to bring back Veronica's humanity in my writing.

Finally, we discuss the issue of the reward and he clarifies for me without any detail that it definitely did not go to Amelia, the female witness. That leaves me intrigued but deciding that it is not a central fact in my story and, even if it were, this ex-cop is not going to divulge the long-held secret. I am inclined to take Ken as a reliable source in this matter.

The time has flown and we have been there for several hours. Ken is very supportive of my project and offers his help with further contacts. Peter takes photos of us all shaking hands and we take our leave. I am so fortunate to have made contact with him. Of all the police involved in the case, Ken was the best person I could have talked to. Bob Giles has died, others are not willing to dig up the past. As we wave and drive off, my head is spinning with the enormous significance and satisfaction of the meeting and I begin to rewrite my book in my head. This interview was worth the entire trip but there is much more to come and an amazing week has only just started.

We now do not have time to go home and freshen up before our evening appointment with our dear friends, Brian and Ruth. They continue to be wonderful role models for us and we love to see them when we are in Adelaide. This time, we do not want them to have to prepare dinner for us, so we are taking them out to eat. The last thing we want to do is to upset our friends by raking up a very distressing event in which they were intimately involved at the time. It must

have been heart-breaking and completely shocking for them when the truth emerged about what had befallen Veronica. They do understand, however, what I am doing and have talked to their family and others who may have small memories of our friend. We chat about old times, discuss current issues, and enjoy a pleasant evening together. Their lives and ours have been full and positive for a very long time since it all happened.

We drive home after a huge and emotional day, and I sleep deeply on the mattress on the floor of our budget bungalow.

Our goal on Tuesday, our second day, is to find the places where Veronica lived and was involved. The first stop is 81 Osmond Terrace in Norwood, previously known as Allambi Hostel. We pull up on the leafy boulevard with the lovely wide median strip and approach the front gate of the graceful double-storey building where we first met Veronica, described in chapter 2. It is now owned by a business, so we photograph from the footpath and over the fence until the receptionist starts to look at us enquiringly. Memories of the gangly teenager flood back and we think of the times we picked her up or dropped her home for events she attended with us.

St Bartholomew's Anglican Church rectory.

Then we take a short drive round the corner up Norwood Parade and recall shopping and eating out there, arriving then in Beulah Road at the beautiful old church, St Bartholomew's Anglican. This was where we first met Brian and Ruth, and where Veronica became a loved member of the community. Our first home as newly-weds was right next door, but that has long gone for a set of units. We take more photos, admire the roses, wander around the church and halls and look at the rectory where she stayed with Brian and Ruth.

Not far away at our next stop, we find what used to be the  Sutherland Lodge Salvation Army Hostel for Girls at 341 Angas Street, East Adelaide. This was Veronica's last home, just 1.8 kilometres from where she was last seen, but rather far to walk home from the city at night. It is a pleasing three-storey building, of wood, not the more common South Australian stone, framed pleasantly with a bed of mauve statice at the front. Now called Angas Lodge, it is a rooming house for men and we see some men coming and going. The plaque that probably had the name of the building has been removed, leaving a space on the front wall. That seems like a metaphor of Veronica's life – all traces gone.

The time has come to drive through the city and out to the Brighton North Cemetery to find her last resting place. We are finally going to Veronica's grave. What took us so long?

20

2017: A Grave

We drive across town to the North Brighton Cemetery, falling silent as we get closer. This is not a place where she used to be: this is where all that is left of her is. I don't know how to feel. I still wonder why we have never looked for this place before on our many trips to Adelaide in the past.

We arrive and drive into the middle of the area, realising that although I have a photo of the headstone, I do not know the number of the plot and neither do we have a map. We stop the car and Peter calls a phone number from an information board and is put through to the historical research person, who turns out to be most helpful. He says that we need to find row 99 and then he would guide us to it. We look up and see that we have stopped exactly in front of that row and I can already recognise the headstone, fifty metres away, on the very edge of the graveyard. Veronica is forever on the margins.

There it is, propped on an uneven angle with two half-bricks taken from the grave next to it (belonging to 'Gertie, from her friends at Minda'). I did know that Veronica is in the 'Minda section' but there is no sign to indicate that, although the current Minda Inc. headquarters is over the road from the cemetery. I cannot believe that we have come all this way and not brought flowers or tools to clean up the plot. It has been a busy week and we are racing from one location to the next, ticking them off my list.

Now I pull up short as we stand there and gaze at the simple stone. We already know there is little information on it but next to the other,

more elaborate graves with names, dates, family members and fond thoughts on them, hers looks stark.

I am not usually a person who takes things that are not mine, but there are plenty of beautiful roses on the bushes near the path, so Peter and I pick a few to lay on the grave, rationalising to ourselves that the flowers will fade tomorrow anyway. That looks better. We take some photos and gaze in contemplation. What is in my husband's head and heart? Graveyards are places to think and reflect and I have mixed feelings. Here lie the remains of our young friend and I feel some sorrow; at the same time, I know she is not here – there is nothing physical left of her remains – and that she is with her Lord. I do not feel the need to cry for her now. I pull out some weeds from the hard ground and tidy around the plot. We have seen what we came to see and we wonder how we can add fuller information to the headstone – for posterity. So that she will not be forgotten any longer. I have no idea that others whom I have not yet even met will become 'Team Veronica' and care for her resting place.

Monday 30 October 2017

Today I hear from Nicola, who tells me that Dorothy wants to visit the grave. How lovely. The chaplain and Nicola will accompany her for support, so the numbers are growing. Some more people to pay their respects to our Veronica.

Monday 13 November 2017

Nicola sends me photos of their visit and the flowers that were put on the grave. I feel so happy knowing that Dorothy, who was Veronica's last 'mother', is now connected to the site and will care for her. I thank God again that we found Dorothy and that she has always cared for her. I hope that her grief will diminish a little, knowing that I am writing for Veronica.

Sunday 3 December 2017

I receive a lovely email from the parole officer I spoke to immediately after our visit to the grave. He and his wife went to visit Veronica's grave. I am so touched by how people have responded to my project, and have gone far beyond lip service. In addition, a stranger at the cemetery who helped them find the grave, visits there every week and has offered to put some flowers on Veronica's grave. He has links with Minda and also wants a copy of the book. This is growing. More importantly, it is so heart-warming to be finding kind and empathetic people everywhere I turn. We have to believe that love wins over evil.

23 January 2018

The additional $100 was donated by the person just bumped into at the cemetery. He told me he has visited the grave three times and has put flowers on her grave.

Veronica is forgotten no more. Her team is growing.

21

1974: A Parolee

Charles Cornwall commenced a new career at the age of thirty-three, after being a government clerk and then an ordained Baptist minister in three churches. He took on the role of a probation and parole officer with the Department of Correctional Services, which gave him the opportunity to use his counselling gifts in supervising adults released into the community from prison on parole or court on supervised good behaviour bonds.

When Cornwall joined the service, there was one central office – in Adelaide – and all the regions, no matter how far away, were serviced periodically by officers from the city. Cornwall was appointed in 1970 to go to a training centre in a little place called Cadell, on the river Murray. It was the pilot in the new push for decentralisation and the appointment of a welfare officer, after some public pressure following abscondings from the low-security prison there. Three years later in 1973, he moved back to the city, where a new phase began, described in his memoirs as 'The Start of my Nightmare'.[45]

In January 1974, Peter and I were married in Melbourne, my hometown, and enjoyed a driving honeymoon that cost us very little but brought us a lot of joy. We arrived back in Adelaide with a few days to settle into our Norwood house before I began my new teaching job in February, and Peter returned to his second year working at McNally Training Centre. We were in our own little world of being newly married after a long wait, broke but happy and busy creating our life together.

A few weeks later, in March 1974, Cornwall was rostered as the duty officer in the Adelaide office. As duty officer, his job was to interview new clients who came from the courts on supervised bonds. On the day in question, one new client was a twenty-year-old young man who had just been sentenced on one count of armed robbery, which had netted him the princely sum of $1.50. His name was Christopher Robin Worrell and he remembers him for having a surprising number of questions about his supervision. Cornwall thought he presented well, was dressed neatly and seemed respectful. It was his first offence and he had no prior convictions, thus his sentence had been suspended and he had been placed under the supervision of a probation officer. Cornwall gathered information about his family, found that he had been reared by his grandmother and had spent three years in the RAAF after he left school; Cornwall fully expected that there would be few problems with this young man.

It was only, however, weeks later that Worrell committed another, more serious, offence of attempted rape and indecent assault, which earned him a four-year sentence and the revocation of the suspension of his previous sentence. Cornwall was to be involved with Worrell for the duration of his time with Correctional Services and it was his job to prepare material for submission to the Parole Board.

Worrell's first application was in November 1975, just seventeen months into his sentence. Cornwall could only find one infringement of prison rules – he had owned a gold earring that was banned and had been disciplined for that. As his parole officer, Cornwall visited his home and spoke with his mother and stepfather, finding the latter to be a strong character and the mother to be gentle. Tellingly, they were not prepared to have Worrell in their home, as they were afraid of him being a bad influence on his teenage brother. Partly because of that, his application was refused. It does seem extraordinary in hindsight that a six-year sentence could have possibly been reduced to seventeen months, given the violence of his crimes.

His second application was deferred when the Parole Board ordered a report from the departmental psychiatrist and also directed Cornwall to obtain a copy of any psychiatric reports from the defence force. Normally difficult to obtain, these were accessed by Cornwall through a helpful contact. There seemed to be no clear recommendations, and eventually the Parole Board released him on 12 October 1976.

In almost the same week, Veronica moved to the Sutherland Lodge Hostel in Angas Street, which was to be her last home. Their lives were about to intersect – violently.

Cornwall's recollections of Worrell's parole period are that his actions and demeanour were unremarkable. He usually reported on a Wednesday night, sometimes in the company of James Miller, who was on a bond and reporting to probation officer John Forrington in the same office. Apart from not turning up to work once and drawing a warning, Worrell's behaviour was satisfactory.

Cornwall heard on 20 February 1977 that Worrell had died in a car accident the day before. Apart from being asked to prevent Miller, who survived the crash, from attending the funeral at Worrell's parents' request, Worrell's history was over and his file closed – for the last time, he thought. 'How wrong, how very wrong I was,' he says ruefully at the end of the first of his two chapters on the case.[46]

The first indication for the parole officer that something terrible had happened on his watch was the media report of the police announcement that was published the day after Miller was arrested, in May 1979. Under the heading 'Car crash victim may have been help', the article in *The Advertiser* was next to the main article about the finding of the bodies. Worrell was named, and a one-line paragraph would have leapt off the page for Cornwall: Worrell 'was on parole when he was killed'. Just as we have experienced in recent years here in my city, in Melbourne, when violent crimes have been committed by a person on parole, there is an inevitable backlash from the public.

Cornwall probably knew what was ahead for him, and it would chase him into his retirement, eclipsing all the other carefully supervised cases and hard work of his career. The outcome of Worrell's horrendous crimes would even call Cornwall's belief in rehabilitation into doubt. Worrell's destruction would have a ripple effect on not only the immediate families of the girls, but on others like this parole officer, who in the course of doing their everyday jobs, were pulled into the vortex of repercussive, ever-widening effects.

> What about all those pre-sentence and parole reports I had written? Had any of them contributed to people being on the streets who should have been in prison?...What about the dreadful Truro murders? Could I have handled things differently? Should I have known what was going on while I was supervising Worrell? Was the criminal justice system in any measure responsible? These questions still haunted me.[47]

It had been difficult for me to find Cornwall's book, as it was not to be found on any of my usual book order sites. Even when I tracked it down in the State Library of Victoria, I had to extract it by special request and have it sent to my local library, where I would need to read it without taking it home. It was engrossing reading and I took notes as I read. On a whim, I did some sleuthing and composed yet another letter – this time to Mr Charles Cornwall; it was posted that same night.

22

2017: An Officer

We drive in through the gates of the retirement community after Charles unlocks it remotely for us. I try to transition in my feelings to the present and marshal my turbulent thoughts. We have come directly from visiting Veronica's grave for the first time and I feel a little vulnerable. As we drive around the curved roadway at the required ten kilometres an hour, I take in the manicured spring gardens that speak of resident garden lovers with some time to care. We watch out for senior citizens and I remind myself that we are now part of this age group for whom we are supposed to drive carefully.

Charles and his wife, both in their eighties, are standing on their path to greet us and I am grateful for their welcoming stance. The assertiveness

I mustered uncomfortably in writing to strangers and asking to speak with them is not my usual style and I am fully aware that this is a sensitive conversation. Who among us has not thought at some time that whoever let a criminal out on parole when a crime was committed must feel bad about it? And Charles is that parole officer. Nevertheless, he has been more than accommodating when we set up this meeting and I have looked forward to talking to him since I read his honest and interesting book of memoirs, *The Punishment Fit the Crime*. The slightly disconcerting lack of an 's' or 'ted' on the end of 'Fit' piqued my imagination and was explained when I realised that it is a line from *The Mikado*. In a strange way, it helped me to feel we would be able to connect, because I am also a Gilbert and Sullivan fan. There are other quotes from Shakespeare and that all sets me at ease. Charles must be a literary and erudite probation and parole officer.

We are ushered in to their cosy unit and Margaret offers us a cuppa. Charles has already flagged that she will be present, and I now feel that it is as much for moral support as for hospitality. Wondering where to find the best place to start, I decide to put Veronica front and centre. I begin to say a few things about her and he leans forward, listening intently. Encouraged, I describe our relationship with her, how she had a circle of loving friends and that she was on her way to visit us. He asks a few questions and Margaret looks sad as I talk; Charles sighs deeply as he enters into our experience and feels again how shocking it was for a young life to have been taken. Talking about Veronica is so different to bundling all the victims together and referring to them as 'seven girls'. I feel warmth and sympathy from him and the interview has begun well. I think he understands why I am doing this and maybe has the first glimmer of something positive emerging from this after the decades of his nightmare. He murmurs affirmation and tells me that he could see from my letter that I am not a nutter. That's comforting.

He has had a few crazies over the years since his terrible realisation and the debate about early parole has raged on and off. In the 3 June edition of *The Sunday Mail* in 1979, it became the 'Issue of the Week', and Justice Roma Mitchell, chairman of the SA Parole Board, defended the parole system after fierce criticism from SA Police Association secretary Mr Ralph Tremethick. He was quoted as saying, 'Today, with our parole system, there is no real deterrent to the crime of murder.' She defended the 'senior parole officer, extremely competent and extremely reliable' and claimed that there were no indicators during the parolee's prison sentence of the spate of criminal behaviour that followed. 'I know some prisoners take parole without the slightest intention of obeying the conditions but how do you judge which ones? You can only do your best.' Which ones indeed?[48]

Charles then brings out an orange folder full of newspaper cuttings and documents. We talk about his book of memoirs and he kindly gives me a copy to keep. Written twenty-four years after the event, it was reviewed in the media, and *The Advertiser*'s well-known crime writer, Nigel Hunt, began his article with the words

Charles Cornwall's conscience is finally clear…the retired probation and parole officer has finally shaken off his feelings of anguish and despair.

He went on to say,

With the stroke of his pen Mr Cornwall could have put Worrell back behind bars and saved the lives of seven victims.[49]

Now Charles reaches into the folder and pulls out a copy of a handwritten letter. I sense this is going to be significant, and he hesitates, his hands shaking a little.

'You can read it, or I can read it out,' he offers. 'It's from Nikki Parrish, the daughter of Deborah Lamb, the last of the victims found.'

She had read the review of his book, and, clearly offended by Nigel Hunt's opening words, she wrote a strong, attacking letter that gutted Charles. Basically, she said that his signature had held her mother's life in its hands. Adopted out as a baby, Nikki had finally made the shocking discovery about the identity of her biological mother. In losing her mum, she also lost any chance of finding out who her father was, and her daughter never knew her grandmother. In addition,

Nikki's grandmother, Rhonda, lost her daughter, Deborah, in horrific circumstances and was understandably affected for the rest of her life. Pain and grief pour off the pages in Nikki's eloquent description of her post-traumatic symptoms, and she ends with 'Merry Christmas, I know mine will never be.' Margaret looks shocked as she listens to the whole letter, and I realise that he has never shown it to her over all these years – for her protection. She is clearly a strong person, and has been his loyal supporter through it all, but he did not want to expose her to this. Tears fill his eyes.

Nikki offered to meet Charles through the victim support service, but he never felt able to do it. Profound sadness fills the room and I wonder where we go from here. I know in my head that the repercussions go on and on from a crime like this but, for the first time, I can feel almost viscerally that we are all victims – or co-victims, as the literature calls us now. Perhaps not as directly wounded as Nikki, but nonetheless still feeling right now the effects of events that happened decades ago. Wrongdoing has far-reaching tentacles and I feel oppression creeping into our meeting. It is as if the effects of a forty-year anaesthesia for Peter and me are wearing off and pain and sensations are emerging from the numbness. I feel Nikki's pain; I feel Charles's pain; I now feel my own sadness as if I never have before.

Then Charles picks up the folder of cuttings and hands it across the room to me. 'You take them,' he says, 'I don't want to keep them any more.'

I pass them to Peter to photograph, but Charles says, 'No, you can have them. I've decided to move on.'

'Are you signing off, Charles?' asks Peter as he takes the bulging folder.

'You could say that.'

We accept the folder as if it is a special gift being entrusted to us. There is a brief silence before the conversation moves on and I understand that something significant has occurred. Margaret is catching up; Charles is letting go; we ourselves are on an unexpected journey. All the circles of direct and indirect victims of this terrible event are somewhere on that journey – we just travel at different speeds.

We talk some more around the parole system and how the various departments and accountabilities changed over the years. Charles explains in detail how probation and parole differ and how, when parole was introduced, the role of probation officer was expanded to include supervision of parolees as well as probationers. He describes how he moved from the Adelaide office to the Norwood office – just around the corner from our first home, the church and Veronica's hostel.

Something strange is happening in this week as I reconstruct a mental map of Adelaide and visualise the key players' movements around the city. When who went where, and the resulting intersections of all of our lives. We didn't know it was happening then, but in my mind I am colour-coding a complex mind map, with new information every day adding to the patterns. For a word person like me, it is unusually and graphically visual and feels indelible.

Charles encourages me to press on and be published – he has had several books printed, from self-publishing to commercial printers – and shares his insights and experience. Finally, I gently refer to his background as an ordained minister, noting the fact that he and Peter had opposite career paths – Peter working in the Correctional Services world before finally becoming an Anglican minister. Charles tells us what I already know from his book: that he does not have faith now; Margaret concurs. I do not want to press our privilege in this conversation and we are quiet again. There is much to ponder.

We take our leave late in the afternoon, still so drawn into the feelings of the visit that this time we forget to take a photo. Talking to Charles and reading Nikki's letter has shown me that I can't pursue this project without touching others and I start to have some misgivings about the effect of another book on those who are still living in pain. My feeling, however, is that it has been positive for us to talk so honestly and I pray that there will be some release for us all. I am learning more every day about the varying journeys of grief and loss, including my own.

23

2017: A Matron

It is now Wednesday 25 October and another clear, warm day – our third in sunny Adelaide. It is as if we are reclaiming our past in this beautiful place, always at its best in spring with flamboyant shows of roses against sandstone and wrought iron. I love this city. We are now feeling at home again, finding our way easily in the simple, orderly grid of main roads, and our little budget bungalow with its challenging eco-toilet has become our temporary home.

This morning, Peter is working on the plaque we will take to Truro later this week. A trip to the hardware store has provided the pickets that we need to secure it into the ground, and Peter is lovingly painting

the routed letters he worked on in our shed before we left home that spell out Veronica's name. We have now seen the people we planned to see and debate together whether to look up some other old friends to fill in these last couple of days. Our instinct is to keep the time open for further developments and agree to stay focused on our mission – and that turns out to be the right call.

I sit down at the desk in the bungalow and reorganise my growing pile of notes and documents. The Report of Missing Person seems precious; the closest connection to Veronica's last night and I decide to trawl through every word to see what further information I can extract from it. Most of what we already knew is confirmed in the report. I note again that it was filed at 2100 hours on Christmas Eve, and realise that it was a busy time for everyone involved, including the police. I slowly read again the description of Veronica, pausing on each word.

Height – 5' 7"; Build – Medium; Hair – Brown; Eyes – brown; Complexion – Fair. [Not as tall as I remember and just an average eighteen-year-old girl. I would have said she was attractive, had a few freckles and a cheeky grin.]

No deformities, peculiarities, moustache or beard, scars or tattoos. [True.]

Blue over-jacket, pink skivvy with yellow flowers on it, blue jeans, brown sandals, gold signet ring right hand, gold earrings. [Who knew exactly what she was wearing? Initially recorded as 'Unknown' and added in handwriting. Probably supplied later by Jenny. Who gave her the ring? I don't know. Her boyfriend? Where is he now?]

Possibly taking Valium. [Why? I didn't know that either.]

Occupation: Invalid pension. [True – she worked at Bedford Industries for very little money, but had over $200 when she went shopping that night.]

Destination unknown. [Not true.]

Cause of absence: Unknown. [True at that time.]

No middle name. No parents' names. [I would like to know these details. I never knew a middle name.]

Date of birth: 14/10/57 – 18 years old. [Not possible for both to be true at the time of the report. She was born in 1958. Even a police record can be incorrect.]

Listed instead of a relative is 'friend' and a scribbled name in the same handwriting as the added clothes description. It looks like Mrs Tait – Sylvia Jean Tait is the Minda nurse who testified at the court case and described Veronica. Who contacted her? We know from one source that Veronica phoned her late on the night she disappeared.

Reported by: D. Reed.

I know that she was the matron of the Salvation Army Hostel. Is she still alive? She is someone I would love to find.

'You've tried to find her, haven't you?' asks Peter as we talk about her.

'Yes, I contacted the Salvation Army national organisation but they had no information or records and could tell me nothing.'

'Why don't you phone the local Salvos and try again?' he suggests.

I baulk at the idea of cold calling with such a complex story and know I would never be given personal information over the phone. Besides, I know the Salvo Southern territory spreads across the continent, and D. Reed could have ended up anywhere from Melbourne to Perth and in between.

'Perhaps we could drop in to divisional headquarters and talk to someone?' is my next thought. I would find it easier face-to-face, and it would be harder to put me off if I am standing at the desk.

Peter already has the address in and it is only five minutes away. We are off on another hunt.

The offices are housed in a beautiful renovated mansion just off Fullarton Road and the receptionist is welcoming. I tell her my rehearsed, short version about why we are looking for a D. Reed, probably a retired officer, and show her the Report of Missing Person.

After looking through a folder she murmurs, 'There is a Major Reed in Adelaide.'

My heart jumps. I suspect she should not have said that.

'But you should probably talk to Nicola. Can you wait a few minutes?'

Nicola comes to the door and takes us to her office – her title is State Director: Salvation Army Family Tracing Service. South Australia Division. Of course. Why hadn't I thought of it before? My mum's last job in the Melbourne office before she retired was in this very department. That's what they do – they find people…

We immediately feel relaxed and I start on my medium-length but succinct version of the story, trying to focus on D. Reed. I start to feel that we are close to something important, but Nicola does not allow me to hurry. She probes gently with just the right questions until suddenly we are pouring out the whole story – the long version. Nicola convinces us that she wants to know all about Veronica and our quest. I don't realise it but Peter tells me later that I change modes and recount it differently to Nicola. Somehow, we are not researching facts but sharing our inside lives with a stranger. My voice cracks once and I pause to regain control. Something has happened in me this week.

'You're still grieving, aren't you?' Nicola asks quietly.

She is right, but I haven't realised it until now. No, no. I can't cry now – we may be on the edge of important new information. Peter takes over the conversation while I find my equilibrium again, but he chokes up too. Sometimes he is more emotional than I am. Nicola makes more notes and says that she may be able to help us, but will have to make some calls. She is reassuring and calm, and she promises to get back to us. I understand that this is her job and that she is very professional. She knows where the boundaries are, but making connections is what she does. What a satisfying job that would be. Nicola shares with us a heart-warming story of one of her successes; it is clear that this is actually more than a job. It does seem that this meeting, although unplanned, may turn out to be one of the most important events on this amazing trip.

Nicola says one more thing as we take photos and exchange details. She asks, 'Have you forgiven Worrell?'

Of course we have. Or have we? Why should we? I need to think about that.

24

2008: A Death

On 21 October 2008, nearly thirty years after the death of his seven victims, James Miller died at sixty-eight years of age. He had hepatitis C related liver cancer, as well as lung and prostate cancer; he was taken to Mary Potter Hospice from Yatala Labour Prison a few days before he died, surrounded by his family. On that day, I was within a few weeks of retiring from my job as principal of an independent school in Victoria, but I did not hear the news, nor have any idea that Miller was close to death.

Sentenced to life imprisonment for the murder of all the girls except Veronica, he initially mounted several unsuccessful appeals. In 1984, he went on a forty-three-day hunger strike and then published his book titled *Don't Call Me Killer*, with assistance from well-known Adelaide crime journalist Dick Wordley. He managed to get a live interview to air with Adelaide radio presenter Jeremy Cordeaux, a television interview with national journalist Jana Wendt and a radio interview with Michael Dodd of 3MP in Melbourne. From within the enclosed confines of prison, he was busy making himself heard. A new law had allowed him to apply for a non-parole period to be set, which was granted for thirty-five years, meaning that he would have been released in 2015. As it was, he was the state's longest-serving prisoner.

In Adelaide, his death was newsworthy, and brought huge relief to some of the victims' families and friends, who were all notified before it was confirmed in the media. For some, like Nikki Parrish, the daughter of Deborah Lamb, the phone call notifying her came as good news, and felt like a birthday present the day after her thirty-third birthday; she felt that a terrible chapter had come to an end. On the other hand, nothing would bring back her mother and the pain would never go away. Julie Mykyta's father also saw Miller's death as the end of an anguished period of thirty years, but felt that it changed nothing for their family.

Thirteen family members made victim statements to the court when Miller applied for the new non-parole period in 1999, but their statements were sealed in an envelope until after his death. So in 2008, they were opened, although the names remained suppressed.

> Convicted serial killer James William Miller has died in an Adelaide Hospice unforgiven, and with the misery he unleashed in the Truro murders still blighting the families of his victims.[50]

Family members described in the statements how their lives had been changed forever, and how they had suffered every day since the deaths and struggled with depression, panic attacks and fear. They were left with lives that were broken and needed psychiatric treatment, and still suffered from sleep disorders, nightmares, emotional instability and even drug abuse. An horrific legacy of pain, mainly carried on the inside, but expressed in varying symptoms of dysfunction and sadness. These were the statements of the immediate family members, but the circle of damage has spread much further for each of the seven victims. Every girl had a wide extended family, a circle of friends, teachers and family friends, neighbours, colleagues, church friends (in Veronica's case) and other acquaintances. Veronica also had the whole extended family of Minda Home friends who mourned her passing, and even today, one can meet staff members and residents from Minda who remember her fondly. And then there is us.

Writing this book has confronted me with the face of evil – which is defined as spoiling goodness – and the magnitude of the loss, grief and fallout from the deeds of two men. James Miller's death brought to an end an era in history, but changed nothing of the events that he and Worrell were responsible for so long ago. They do not deserve to be forgiven and they never asked for it – in Miller's book, there is absolutely no sign of remorse for his part in the crimes – although it has to be acknowledged that they both also suffered at the hands of others, whether in their families or in institutions.

Why is it that the broken will break others? Why do some victims become perpetrators and deny their own moral compasses? And more importantly, how do we who are also victims ensure that we do not perpetuate that cycle by passing on our own damage? I have heard Rwandan people seeking to right the horrific wrongs of genocide in their country say, 'Forgiveness is for me.' I believe there is truth in that. The more we are able to forgive rather than judge, the more whole we become, and are empowered to cut the ties in order to live in freedom and grace. But there is more than just me: if we do not forgive, we risk passing on the damage and burden to the next generation. Those whom we love need to receive hope and honesty from us, and the power to forgive is at the centre of that dynamic. It is our responsibility to bring the flow of destruction to a stop. For me personally, it is a spiritual issue and I need God's help.

25

2017: Forgiveness

After the previous day's developments at the Family Tracing Service office, we drove down to the beach, where we walked, talked and cleared our heads. Fresh air, sea views and no agendas. A delicious Chinese meal and contact with our family. I don't think they have entered yet into understanding what on earth we are doing here in Adelaide. Something to do with that book about serial killers that Mum is writing…

While we were on the road, I received a warm email from Charles, the former parole officer whom we met on Tuesday. He wrote,

> Margaret and I were so pleased to meet with you and Peter yesterday and hear of your plans for Veronica's book. When I received your first letter I was convinced that what you were doing was a positive and good thing, though my reasons for coming to that conclusion were somewhat vague at the time. Now that we have met and you have explained in more detail your motivation and aims, and told me more about Veronica herself and what she was actually doing at the time she was accosted, my original rather nebulous feelings of approval have now been given real substance and, for what it's worth, I want you know that you have my total support.
>
> As I see it, what your book will do is give a face, a person, to what was just a name. And a name that, in many people's minds, is synonymous with that of a loose woman walking the streets 'looking for it'. I now know, and what others will learn through your book is that, in Veronica's case at least, this could not be further from the truth. I have to say that when I heard the

story of Veronica I felt deeply saddened. I lay awake for several hours thinking of this innocent young girl, full of life, happily planning for her trip to Melbourne, buying presents (perhaps for you), only to have her life snatched away in such a terrifying and brutal manner, I just felt indescribably sad. What is worse, she has become just a name. A person of no importance in a pauper's grave. A nobody's girl. This must be rectified and your book will help.

Charley

I shed a few tears and realised that even if the book were never published, my mission was beginning to succeed and Veronica was being remembered at last. I was also extremely grateful that Charles was expressing his support. He had every reason never to want to think about the event again.

Today, Thursday, is our last full day in Adelaide and I wonder how it will unfold. We do a few jobs, feeling as though we need to be in good shape for whatever happens today. And happen it does. I am sitting at my laptop catching up on my journal entries when the phone call from Nicola comes. She has found Major D. Reed, a retired Salvation Army officer living close by, but she is too distressed to talk to us. I am elated and disappointed, all at once. How wonderful that the D. Reed who reported Veronica to be missing, is alive and residing here in Adelaide. It is sobering to realise that this contact out of the blue after forty years has upset her and I am reminded yet again that others are not on the same journey as I am; it is not necessarily a joyful thing to hear from me. I have been reprocessing this for a year – could I expect her to do a fast-forward catch up in one hour?

The good news is that Nicola has asked her the questions that she imagines I would want to and passes on the answers over the phone. I am very grateful for that. Major Reed would like to visit the grave soon and Nicola, ever pastoral, has arranged for a chaplain to visit her.

We learn through Nicola's account of the phone conversation about how Veronica came to the hostel after working as a companion for the elderly lady in her home. Major Reed sends her love to us and is praying for us. I ask if I may know her first name. It is Dorothy. Bless you, Dorothy. You cared for our girl. Not everyone has forgotten Veronica. I determine that I will be happy with this unexpected contact, but questions are flooding into my mind.

We need to go yet again to the mega hardware store – Peter needs some longer stainless steel screws to attach the pickets to the plaque and he forgot to bring a spade for our Truro planting. Our time in Adelaide is running down very quickly.

'Peter, when we go out, do you think we could drop in to another cemetery?'

He looked at me enquiringly.

'I can't get Nicola's question out of my mind and I would like to go to Worrell's grave. I think we need to make our peace before we go to Truro tomorrow.'

I am beginning to understand that if my research into Veronica's murder just increases my anger and grief, then there is no point. If it helps me to work through and deal with suppressed feelings and unresolved sadness, then it will not only give Veronica a voice, but my voice might be used to help others caught up in this dreadful saga. It is time to do something I had never thought of doing – forgiving is the only way to draw a line under a profoundly damaging event.

I know from my internet searches that Worrell's grave is in the Centennial Park Cemetery. My focus thus far has been stubbornly fixed on Veronica, the other girls and the background of the events. I have tried not to focus on either the horrific events or the perpetrators, except as they interacted with Veronica's story. Now, thanks to Nicola's care for us, I know that this is something that Peter and I need to do to be released from the darkness that I have opened up to write this story. Just as the grief has been buried for so long, so has the anger, however justified it might be. Both have been uncovered this week and we are in need of healing if we are to recover our emotional and spiritual health out of this journey. In addition, my quest has reopened wounds for others – especially Charles and Dorothy – and potentially a much wider circle if the book gains traction. We are all victims, even so many years later, and I feel as if we need to say a few things to a dead murderer and his accomplice on behalf of all of us.

While we are cruising around the cemetery looking for the grave, Nicola phones me again with exciting news: Dorothy would now like to meet us. Are we free today? We certainly are! This is the person I have longed to meet since this quest began, and somehow between our hunting and Nicola's help, it is going to happen. I am thrilled and stunned all at once; we arrange to meet at the Salvation Army offices at 3 p.m. Right now, it is important that we find Worrell's grave, and we do. We are on a roller coaster of emotions, but just go with the ride.

'Untold joy and love he brought to all'. It is shocking, particularly for Peter, who has not seen the photo of the grave, to see these words on the plaque in the lawn cemetery for Christopher Robin Worrell. Even his given names are hauntingly ironic, referencing the given names of a childhood innocent favourite. No one, of course, apart from Miller knew of his crimes when he was buried in February 1977. His family mourned his premature death, as would any family whose son died so young in a car accident. They are also victims in this tragedy, especially when the truth emerged of the damage wrought by their son. Miller grieved for the only real friend he had and hid a note in the grave the night before (which the police later retrieved by exhuming Worrell's coffin).

Other plaques all surround and adjoin Worrell's engraved headstone. Do the families visiting those memorials realise that their relatives are lying in graves beside a serial killer?

We gaze at the plaque, and then look out at the glorious view across the manicured lawn. We both speak out aloud to Worrell. We tell him of lives cut short and families destroyed – including his. We tell him how much anger and grief has been generated by his heinous deeds and that we have every right to be angry and sad too. We try to articulate the pain that he caused. Peter feels like reaching into the grave, pulling Worrell out by the scruff of the neck to have this talk. We fall silent and then hand it all over to God and forgive Veronica's killers – we refuse to live in that anger. We haven't arrived at this place easily but we take comfort in having the assurance that the worst thing cannot happen to her or to us. Nothing can separate us from the love of God – not death, nor violence, nor grief.

As we walk back to the car, I realise that I feel somehow refreshed and re-energised, almost as if I have been turned inside out. I want my story to be a power for good, as well as telling about Veronica's life and death, and I understand now how this experience in the cemetery today will affect my writing. We never just write words; they are always dynamically laden with experiences and feelings.

Peter crosses the busy road beside the cemetery to the florist to buy flowers for our meeting with Dorothy and I marvel at how all these momentous events have fallen into place in exactly the right order. It could not have been orchestrated any better in this week of discovery.

26

2017: Dorothy

If there were one person I would have liked to find this week before we went home to Melbourne, it would be Dorothy; I just cannot believe that we are on our way to meet her now. We wait in the reception area of the Salvation Army building until Nicola takes us into a quiet room set up with a tablecloth and flowers on the table. Yet another beautiful afternoon tea as the setting for uncovering the memories of events from forty years ago. As they are revealed, will there be release?

And here is Dorothy at last. She is almost eighty years old, but is sprightly in her Salvo uniform and has a gentle smile and soft, silver hair. I have changed my clothes after a busy day and put on make-up for this event – we all know this is a significant and special meeting and want to look our best. We give her the flowers and all embrace each other with long hugs. At this moment, I am not writing a book; I am meeting Veronica's last 'mum', who loved her and cared for until the end. It is still hard to take it in but we savour the moment. Nicola looks on quietly, pouring tea, hovering and ready to look after Dorothy but not intruding. We owe Nicola a great debt of gratitude for this almost sacred moment.

Sitting at the round table, we talk for over an hour, sharing our stories and filling in the gaps. I am almost too engrossed to write anything but see that Peter is also taking notes. We hear the details about how Veronica came to the hostel and was well accepted by the other girls in spite of, or even because of, her disability. Dorothy tells us that she kept her room beautifully tidy, liked to sew, dressed smartly and looked after herself. She knows that she had friends at the church.

We are interested to learn about the Sutherland Lodge Hostel, which was home for forty-two girls from the country who were studying or working and needed somewhere secure to live. They paid $25 per week each for their board, which was not a small sum in those days. Dorothy and her assistant, Loretta, ran the whole place with a little help from volunteers so that they could have a few hours to themselves in a day. Dorothy tells us that she was up at six every morning to cook a good breakfast for the girls. She speaks fondly of her charges and it is clear that she worked way beyond set hours to look after them. Dorothy was the matron at Sutherland Lodge for ten years from 1972, having trained in the Salvation Army training college in 1962–4 as part of the cohort named Servants of Christ. That seems to be an appropriate description for this retired matron who has served many people in her lifetime.

It is painful for Dorothy, who was thirty-eight at the time, to recall the events of that night. Over forty years later, she describes seeing Veronica and Jenny hanging up their keys on the way out. We know she is remembering her last glimpse of Veronica. She cautioned them that night knowing that it would be a busy shopping night with crowds in the city, told them not to talk to people and to look after their belongings and money. The girls were excited and happy as they headed out on that summer night.

At 10 p.m., Jenny came home alone and Dorothy describes how she was immediately worried when Veronica was not home by curfew time at 11.30 p.m. Dorothy remembers thinking about the fact that Veronica had never been late before. She talked to her assistant and they decided not to speak to the other girls yet but to try to track her down. She went to Veronica's room and found her address book, and began to call all her friends with an Adelaide number, even though it was getting late in the evening. She hoped that Veronica was staying somewhere and had forgotten to phone her. No one had heard from her. She did not call us; we were listed in the book but were too far away in Melbourne – she could not have gone that far in a couple of hours. She must have called Brian and Ruth sometime that night or the next day, as they then let us know about Veronica's disappearance.

I am hanging on every word as she speaks – the gaps in the story are being filled by the only person who could possibly know, and we are in the same room as her. She did not talk to the other girls because she did not want to frighten them. I am sure, however, that Jenny must have talked. How was she feeling?

Dorothy then tells us about reporting the absence to the police and being sent away because it was too early. She had to wait twenty-four hours, but she went back the next night, on Christmas Eve. She was busy with Christmas events, but returned before the twenty-four hours was up and filed the report by 9 p.m. She says that she persisted and went back every day to ask for news but there was none. The police came to the hostel and told her to lock the room, not to touch anything and to leave it as it was. It was a constant reminder to her, as were the detectives who came to see her from time to time – but never with any news. She also reminisces about later events when the media continued to want access to Veronica's room.

There was so much to do on Christmas Day. Apart from attending a church service, there was the festive lunch to prepare for the girls who remained in the hostel. Their tradition was to play a friendly footy match in the afternoon and just have fun together. This year there was a pall hanging over the group and the girls were asking questions, so Dorothy finally had to talk with them. There were, no doubt, tears and hugs as the awful possibilities became apparent. It was perplexing and frightening for them all as the hours ticked by and there was no sign of their friend.

Dorothy then tells us more confronting aspects of her story. A few months later, her grief was compounded when another of her girls was abducted and brutally assaulted. Once again, she was back at the police station to report the missing girl, and the sadness of losing Veronica was aroused again for her. In addition, she had some difficult situations in her family around that time and was carrying heavy burdens of her own. It sounds as though it was a very traumatic time for her and we ask her how she managed to carry on. She tells us about the strength of her faith in God and the support of a wonderful mentor. I ponder the use of the modern word 'mentor' and am grateful that someone helped her through a dreadful and lonely time. No wonder she feels distress in recalling it all. I feel some regret to have aroused her memories, yet hope that our connection today will have a positive outcome for us all. I am certain of one thing: this meeting was meant to be.

I am very aware of the need to tread carefully now, so we skirt around the news of the discovery of Veronica's remains and the actual events – there is plenty of information in the public space. I don't want Dorothy to think about all of that again, and I probably know more than she does by now. She talks again about how the media pestered her for photos and film of the room at the hostel; she refused and guarded the room. As the awful truth began to emerge, the media was flooded with Truro developments and all of Adelaide was well aware of the tragedy. Dorothy's lost girl became the centre of a national drama.

We jump forward to Miller's trial, and Dorothy discloses a hugely significant fact: she went to the Supreme Court trial every single day. All these years I have wished that we could have been there to represent Veronica and have mourned the fact that she seemed largely forgotten. The other six families all were present and well documented in the media. There were convictions for the crimes against their daughters, but not for Veronica. Now we are hearing that Dorothy was there for her. I feel a deep happiness as I hear this for the first time in these forty years and just want to hug Dorothy. It has been worth all the work to discover this. She describes where she sat at the trial – a couple of metres from Miller in the dock. She could almost have touched him, and she says that she stared at him most of the time. How disappointed she must have been when the verdict for her girl was 'not guilty'. Now four decades have slipped past. And I turn up out of the blue.

This is the story we have needed to hear and I hope it has helped Dorothy to hear our part in Veronica's life. We chat about our happy times with her and fill in the earlier years for Dorothy. She didn't know where the grave is but will now go to visit it as we have, and I know it will bring both sadness and peace.

We talk some more as we finish our drinks, and there are two more pieces that are special in this jigsaw puzzle of which I have somehow become a part. When I tell Dorothy about my Salvo family background, her eyes light up to hear my parents' names (they were officers or ministers, like her). She, of course, knew them. She said my dad was 'very tall', and my mum was 'lovely'. That makes me feel as if Dorothy is a long-lost aunt.

Moreover, Nicola has her own revelation in this adventure. She contacted Major Reed to set up the meeting, and when they met, she discovered that she had known her all along. Nicola and Dorothy are both volunteers at a Friday fund-raising market, and Nicola calls her 'Dot' or a fun nickname, 'Bag Lady', because she always has bags of goods for the market. She never knew her full name until today and realised that Dot and Major Reed are the same person. There are reunions all round. This whole project has laid bare the unexpected intersections of our lives, which add to the warmth and human connection.

An amazing coda will emerge later: Nicola discovers that her father-in-law, Harry, was the officer-in-charge of the mounted police involved in the search at Truro, and found the third and fourth bodies. Another incredible piece of the puzzle.

The afternoon has flown by and the office is closing. We take some photos and share more long hugs all round. How can someone I have known for just over an hour feel like a family member? I promise Dot and Nicola a copy of the book each and perhaps a digital photo book to celebrate Veronica's life. My list of people who will receive the book – that I have still to write – is growing and I realise yet again that not finishing it is now not an option. I feel as if we are being propelled along a road that just keeps turning corners at the right time.

27

2017: A Pilgrimage

It will be thirty-four degrees centigrade with a north wind in Adelaide today, perhaps similar to the weather on 23 December 1976. Today we leave Adelaide and will undertake a pilgrimage to the bush on our way back to Melbourne after a momentous week of discoveries about Veronica's life and death. We pack up and check out, loading our suitcases and some extra things into the boot of the car – a potted mauve flowering bottlebrush (callistemon Mauve Mist), a bag of potting mix, a sledgehammer, a cheap spade from Bunnings, and the twenty-litre plastic container of water we brought from our own tanks in Melbourne. Most importantly, we have the wooden plaque that Peter has made and etched to mark the spot where Veronica was found. We point the car in the direction of the road north to Truro and begin our drive.

We are quiet as we reach the main Gawler road and realise that it will take us at least an hour. I am reluctant to think about it, but cannot help wondering if, forty years ago, Veronica was alive on this trip. What about the other girls? It is as if we cannot avoid following her to the end if we are truly to be released from all that we have entered into this week. Miller gave two differing accounts of what happened on that night, so we will probably never know the truth. If they drove from the hills, they might well have taken another scenic route to Truro that bypasses the city. It would have been dark that night, but today as we drive, it is not yet noon and the heat is shimmering over the waving wheat fields that stretch to the horizon on both sides of the freeway.

Somehow, I imagined that Truro would be a run-down little town, but it surprises us. Named after a town in Cornwall, it is part of the 'Cornish triangle' north of Adelaide – coincidentally, an area of interest to me as the region to which my own Cornish forbears migrated in the mid nineteenth century. Complete with a huge paved parking area for trucks and caravans, it is clearly the favoured stopping place on the run from the city to the Riverland.

The bakery in the main street has a line of people spilling out the door, with pastries and cold drinks obviously the popular choice. We are caught up in the crowded shop with a bus-load of kids with disabilities spending their $10 notes that are held safely in snap-lock bags, each taking an age to decide which coloured doughnut they will choose. They are having so much fun, but I feel sober knowing that we are near our dark destination – these kids actually remind me of Veronica.

Peter takes a walk to the post office to see if anyone knows any details about the site we are looking for, but forty years is too long ago. So much is now forgotten and even the town of Truro has moved on from its infamous history. People all know about Truro but no one has the details.

I wonder how we are going to find the exact spot, let alone get access to it. Peter suggests contacting the Nuriootpa Police Station, from where the search was managed. I doubt that anyone can help us but decide to call the number anyway. A pleasant female voice answers and I try to make my enquiry as brief but clear as possible – no easy task.

'My name is Jeanette and I'm in Truro wanting to find a spot in the bush where the bodies of the Truro murder victims were found in 1978 and 1979. We had a close relationship with one of the girls and would like to pay our respects at the spot where her remains were discovered. Is there anyone at the station who might know, or are there any records? It was the first body found that we're interested in.'

It is so hard to frame the question with enough information but not too much. There is a pause.

'Can you hold for a moment?' she says. 'I might be able to help you. You want the location of the first body?'

'That's right,' I confirmed, suddenly a little hopeful.

We pull over to the side of the road as we wait, and a few minutes later, she returns and says, 'You drive sixteen kilometres from Truro along the highway to Swamp Road. There's a sign there. Turn down the road and exactly a kilometre on the left is the spot.'

I could not believe it. We had come this far with only approximate locations surmised from various blurred photos and sketch maps, thinking that we would have to be satisfied with a notional spot, and now, minutes before we arrive, someone is telling us the exact location. Did she consult a file or did someone at the station know? We should not be surprised. The whole week has been like this – perfect timing for each revelation. Good suggestion, Peter.

We do a U-turn and drive the sixteen kilometres east from Truro in silence and stop at the intersection. There is, in fact, no sign – even the name of the road is forgotten. It is, however, Swamp Road and we turn the car and look down it.

'I am so glad you came with me on this trip. I don't think I could have come here on my own,' I say to Peter.

'Of course you couldn't,' he replies. 'We had to come together to do this.'

Once again, I am reminded that what started out as my book project has turned into our pilgrimage together. Our journey of discovery, of forgiveness and now, memorial. In a way we could never have anticipated, it has become a gift to us and, we hope, to some other people still touched by an event almost forgotten.

We drive slowly down Swamp Road. This was Veronica's last journey, whether she was dead or alive.

It is, not surprisingly, exactly as we have seen it on Google Earth. An unmade road of red dirt with patches of scrubby bush either side. I note with dismay the tightly strung barbed wire fence on both sides. What will we do? I am not particularly nimble and it is too high to climb over and too closely strung for us to fit between the barbs. Nine hundred metres on the speedometer. It is close. We slow down to a crawl and then see it. There is a broken fence post that has fallen down and taken the wire down with it onto the stony dirt. It is exactly at the kilometre mark. Can this be true?

After driving further down the length of the dusty road, we come back to the spot and park on the edge of the road. Peter holds down the springy post and wire and I make it safely over, carrying the spade. We are here – I recognise the shape of this group of trees from the maps we have examined. What a strange, open place to dump bodies! There is far denser bush quite close by, but I realise again that I cannot attempt to get into the mind of a psychopath.

Will anyone mind if we plant our memorial here? We do not know but are certain that we have to do it. It is a native plant and will not be invasive. There is some patchy shade where a few trees cluster and we choose a spot that might be sheltered enough to give the shrub a reasonable chance at surviving. When Peter has heaved the rest of the equipment in over the fence, I try digging the spade into the baked red earth – it is hard but crumbles as the shiny edge cuts in. This will be hard work. I wonder what a passer-by may think if they see us digging a big hole in this forsaken place.

We don hats and sunscreen and it takes Peter a while to dig a hole large enough for the roots of our plant.

In the searing heat, he shouts out to the silent bush as he digs, 'Planting something living, Veronica, for you. You're with the God of the living and the dead, and there's a very close space between heaven and earth.' He is sweating as he digs and yells into the simmering noon heat.

There are no words for what I am feeling and thinking.

We pour in water and potting mix, settling the roots of the plant into the gaping hole. We backfill with more water and mix the red dirt

with some potting mix. The bottlebrush looks at home there, but there is no other green growth apart from a few tiny weeds struggling up out of the dry soil. For no special reason, like a good gardener, I add the plant label behind it. Next, we hammer in the plaque on its star pickets, slightly cracking the wood in the process. 'Veronica. Psalm 23' becomes the backdrop for the callistemon.

I photograph each stage and gaze around, looking across the road

to where two more bodies were found, and over the back towards the highway, where another was discovered. Then down to the south where Miller, on the night of his arrest, took the police to find the last body.

Returning to the car and brushing red dirt from our clothes and shoes, we head east, feeling free to head home. The sky is dramatically wide in the bush and we can see a dark weather front in the sky coming behind us. Will rain fall on the young bottlebrush that will reach its roots and encourage growth? We have to leave it behind us now, and in doing so, lay it all down.

The heavy storm cloud swings around to the south and overtakes us as we speed along the highway; suddenly a beautiful rainbow appears like an arch framing the road ahead. The very first rainbow signified hope and promise and, to our amazement, this one lasts nearly two hours, hanging right over where we are heading. We feel enveloped by its luminous beauty and drive towards it, embraced by its arc. We are at peace, with Veronica held in our hearts until we meet again.

Appendix

A discussion of some questions arising from this story

How much of the responsibility lay with the Parole Board?

In posing this question, it is important to distinguish between the Parole Board and the parole officers who make their reports to the board.

The Parole Board

In South Australia, when the first parole laws were passed in 1969 until 1981, the board carried the heavy responsibility of making decisions about prisoners' parole release dates and the conditions for their release. It comprised a committee of five people, led by a chairperson 'with extensive knowledge of, and experience in, the science of criminology, penology or any other related science'. Under these provisions, unless the court had specified a minimum 'non-parole' term – which in practice it rarely did – most prisoners become eligible to be considered for parole immediately they were sentenced.[51] This does explain why Worrell managed to be released on parole only twenty-seven months into a six-year sentence – today that seems manifestly inadequate given the violent nature of his offences.

In 1981, when Miller was in prison, there was a legislated change to the Prisons Act that affected his sentencing and caused him to apply for a new non-parole period to be set for his life sentences – he received thirty-five years, taken from 1980, meaning that he would have been released in 2015 had he lived that long. It should be noted that in this change, South Australia moved from what is known as an *indeterminate* mode of parole to a *determinate* mode. While the latter gives the court the sole responsibility in deciding the length of the sentence to be served in prison before release on parole, the indeterminate style operated in 1976 in Worrell's case: offenders would only be released when experts decided that they were rehabilitated and thus not likely to offend again. Miller's incarceration fell later in the determinate era.

In December 1983, a number of amendments were introduced in the parliament in response to prisoner unrest and major riots in Yatala Prison over perceived unfairness in enacting the new parole laws. These amendments were passed speedily and the board now had little or no power to grant or refuse parole. In this new phase, its function became essentially to 'set and monitor conditions to be observed by offenders on parole and to institute breach proceedings where appropriate'.[52] The non-parole period had now gone from being the minimum time a prisoner had to serve, to the maximum, less any remissions granted. This system has continued to the present day.

Parole and probation officers

As has already been noted in an earlier chapter, probation and parole officers functioned in a dual capacity, supervising both offenders discharged from court on supervised good behaviour bonds and those released from prison on parole. With regard to parole, the officer had two main responsibilities in the relevant period of 1969–1981. The first was investigating and reporting to the board on the applicant's suitability for parole, including prison reports, accommodation and employment prospects and plans, and the desirability of alcohol and/ or drug treatment. The second came into play when the prisoner was released on parole and included monitoring the offender's compliance with parole conditions and acting in a social work capacity in advising and assisting the parolee. Worrell did not put a foot wrong while he was in Yatala Prison – apart from once wearing a prohibited gold earring – and all the information in his file would have testified to his good record. The parole officer's further responsibility was to 'supervise' the parolee when he left prison and to ensure that he or she kept the conditions of the parole period. Worrell's first application for parole was on 25 November 1975, after having served only seventeen months of his sentence. As detailed in Cornwall's book of memoirs, it was refused on 9 December after it was ascertained that his parents were not prepared to receive him back at home and reported accordingly to the board.

His second application was in June 1976, and this time Mr Cornwall added to his report a suggestion that reports be sought from the air force to follow up Worrell's story of an alleged brain clot and the reason for his dismissal from the forces. With some difficulty, the board obtained confidential psychiatric and psychological reports, in addition to a medical examination carried out that revealed a dysrhythmia. They considered all of this on 12 July, 3 and 27 September, resulting in his release on parole on 12 October 1976.

His parole conditions were that he was required to continue in pre-arranged employment as a presser in a dry-cleaning shop near his grandmother's place, which had been arranged for him by the industry officer in charge of the dry-cleaning workshop at Yatala. He was required to live with his maternal grandmother at Edwardstown, abstain from alcohol (because of his heart dysrhythmia) and report weekly to his parole officer; this usually happened on a Wednesday evening after work. Often at the same time, Miller, who was on a good behaviour bond, would report to Probation Officer Forrington's office in the same building. Cornwall obtained another job for Worrell in early November when he lost his job through non-attendance, but had no cause for concern through the period of supervision, until he was notified of his death in the accident on 19 February.[53]

Four years after Miller was convicted and incarcerated, the newspapers reported after an episode of *Sixty Minutes* (aired on 4 March 1984 on Channel 9) that hope of parole had been mentioned by Miller. At that stage, he had no minimum period on his life sentence; under the new parole legislation he would have to return to a sentencing court to have a non-parole period set, which he later did. This publicity in the press brought a strong response from the attorney-general of the time, Mr Sumner, who reassured the anxious public and the victims' families that there was no possibility of Miller being released.

Soon after the conclusion of the committal trial in 1979, criticism was aired by Mr Ralph Tremethick, the secretary of the Police Association, causing Chairman Justice Roma Mitchell to reply through the media. Addressing his demands that the workings of the board be made public, she made the point that the parole system was not within the working conditions of police officers, who would have had no contact with prisoners since before they went to prison. Noting that the board sat for only half a day every fortnight, she acknowledged that it was difficult to interview each applicant personally, but that the request of prison officers had been heard and they now had lists of those applying for parole so that they could observe them more closely. She explained that in Worrell's case, there were no red flags in the system when he applied and nothing that the parole officer could have told the board. It was also explained that a parolee was under supervision for the rest of his sentence time, which could be the rest of his life.

Even with hindsight, it would seem that normal procedure was followed in the case of Christopher Worrell. In July 1979, the South Australian parliament was reassured by the chief secretary in a written account answering questions from Mr Wilson, the opposition transport minister.

The issue arose again in 1980 in the media after the evidence given by Miller at his trial became public. In the 'Letters to the Editor' of an Adelaide newspaper, C.T. Moodie queried how a man such as Worrell could be 'free to roam the streets of Adelaide at night', and proposed increasing the police force in order to supervise parolees more closely out of hours. W. Allan Rodda replied two days later on behalf of the Parole Board, and pointed out that twenty-four-hour supervision was never envisaged. This brought a reply from Moodie four days later, requesting transparency, backed up by C.G. Kerr, who observed that the system of sentencing courts and the board seemed to be working against one another. The last letter in this series is from none other than T.C. Coulthard, the juror who spoke publicly after the trial and assisted Miller with his book. He is adamant in his letter that the Parole Board have to 'share the blame for the tragedy which followed'. I tend to agree with him – the system was flawed. These days we speak of the 'pub test': there is no doubt that Worrell's early release would not have passed that test now.

One further issue may be relevant in answering this question. In 1981, the *Royal Commission into Allegations in Relation to Prisons under the Charge, Care and Direction of the Director of the Department of Correctional Services and Certain Related Matters* took place. Some of the 'matters' examined were prison administration and personnel. A media report on the commission mentions in passing Worrell's psychiatrist report that was requested before he was granted parole. Clive Humphrey, a prisoner, also gave evidence that Worrell had told him that Worrell had blackmailed the psychiatrist concerning 'sexual matters' to manipulate the system to his own advantage. In addition, he gave anecdotal evidence of further misdemeanours allegedly carried out against another prisoner's daughters. Humphrey also produced in evidence a letter from the attorney-general that acknowledged his claims about the said psychiatrist, and alleged that he was known by the police and the medical board. Nonetheless, there would be no action taken against him in the interests of all concerned.

The level of credibility for all of this is difficult to determine, but suffice to say it was all duly recorded as part of the Royal Commission and made public. To draw together the strands of my discussion, these are the factors with regard to Worrell's early release:

1. It was part of the normal parole procedure of the time, and in line with the provisions of the law between 1969 and 1981. The system later changed.
2. The parole and probation officers at that time were required to report on the prisoner's behaviour during incarceration and their expressed desire to reform such behaviour. After the parolee was

released into the community, he was required to report weekly, and keep the conditions of the parole. The officer did what was necessary to oversee this compliance, but this did not involve round the clock surveillance.

3. Prison officers had little say in the report and often did not even know which prisoners were applying to the board. This also was changed after Worrell's time and lists were provided to the prisons.

4. The police were barely involved in matters of parole and were not represented on the board. Once prosecution succeeded and people were sentenced, they were not the concern of the police until after release. Even then, it was never envisaged that they should be under surveillance.

5. The Parole Board at the time of Worrell's release bore the major responsibility for parole decisions when they made the final decision. They were, however, dependent on the information given to them, were under-resourced and unable even to interview many applicants face-to-face. The situation is still the same today, and being on the board requires many hours of intensive reading in the members' own time. If the reports they received were flawed, or even corrupted, as is possible in the case of Worrell's medical reports, they had no way of knowing.

In summary, I believe the system was very unwieldy and board decisions could be influenced by factors no one could control. When we add a manipulative and scheming prisoner like Worrell, who knew how to ensure that he would be released by the board, we have a perfect storm.

In addition, there are those who believe that a longer sentence will not reform a person with malevolent intent, and that is possibly true for Worrell. If he had been released later, or even served his whole sentence, we cannot know that he would have acted any differently. Veronica might still be alive, and another six families not still be in grief, yet there is every possibility that the murders might have been perpetrated on a different set of victims.

When we add Miller's assistance and his probable involvement, it is clear that many factors might converge to bring about events that are good or evil. That conclusion is of little comfort to those of us who lost a daughter or friend, but it has to be acknowledged.

Was Miller's trial a mistrial?

While there is little doubt that Miller was guilty at the very least of being deeply involved in the criminal enterprise of murder, a question arose at the time as to whether the verdict was the result of a mistrial. Miller's legal team claimed that Justice Matheson had wrongly advised the jury when he answered the final question from them before the verdict was returned.

One of the most important points in the entire trial was the interpretation of the concept of 'joint criminal enterprise' and whether Miller was as guilty as Worrell was for his part in the events. He had always claimed that he only drove the car and assisted in disposing of the bodies. After retiring at 1 p.m., the jury came back into the courtroom several times and finally for further clarification of this issue at 9.01 p.m. on the last night of the trial. Justice Matheson's explanation to them finished with these words:

> If you are satisfied beyond reasonable doubt that the accused and Worrell were acting in concert to pick up a girl and that the accused drove Worrell and that girl to Truro or somewhere else and it was within the contemplation of Miller that that particular girl may be murdered, he is guilty of murder.

The critical change from his opening statement to the trial was that he had previously used the word 'would' be murdered instead of 'may' be murdered – and that difference brought the jury back very quickly at 9.18 p.m. with a verdict. (Some accounts use the word 'might', but the meaning is the same.) As would later be pointed out by a juror, one T.C Coulthard, the jury were left with little choice, as the word 'may' increased the probability factor to include all the events after Veronica was killed (based on the assumption that Miller could not have known that Veronica would die). Mr Coulthard claims that had the word 'would' been retained, the jury could not have agreed on the verdict, let alone so quickly. He felt strongly enough to write to Miller's lawyers about the matter, although he was not questioning Miller's guilt, but rather the integrity of the legal process.

When an appeal was lodged on this basis, it was rejected by two out of three of the sitting judges – Chief Justice King, who headed the group, considered that the direction to the jury by Matheson amounted to a miscarriage of justice, and that there had been an oversimplification of the issue. Dick Wordley explored the issue in his addendum to Miller's book, and quoted from Justice King's words in the transcript of the appeal:

> The result, in my opinion, has been to deny to the appellant that which the law guarantees to him and to every citizen charged with crime, namely a fair trial according to law. With all respect to my brethren who think otherwise, it seems to me that that denial amounts to a substantial miscarriage of justice.[54]

One can only ponder what direction the trial would have taken had a new trial been called. At the very least, both this legal argument and the veracity of Amelia's testimony would have been scrutinised further, and the outcome might have been different.

It is also worth noting that the change in wording probably made no difference to the lack of a conviction for Veronica's death, as the argument would have been that Miller could not have known whether she 'would', or 'might' have died unless his involvement was much greater than he admitted.

Was the police response to the case adequate?

This is one of the questions that prompted me to revisit and review this whole event. From a distance (we were overseas at the time and for several years afterwards), it appeared that Veronica's disappearance was not taken very seriously and that there was not much evidence of steps being taken to track her down.

From my own point of view, I have never understood why we were not contacted in Melbourne when it was known that her train ticket (found in her room) had been purchased in order to travel to visit us two days after her disappearance. We were her next destination and our name and address were known to the hostel staff, as evidenced by it being recorded on the missing person report filed by the matron.

There has never been any reference to whether the hotel staff at the door of the Majestic Hotel and surrounding shops were questioned. If Miller's story is true, the two men frequently picked up girls in King William Street and their appearance was distinctive enough to be remembered – a long-haired youth, accompanied by an older man who drove a white car. I would have thought that questioning people who might have been present when she disappeared would be standard police procedure.

Our friends, Brian and Ruth, were concerned enough to ask for help from Detective Len Brown, a member of the church in Norwood where Veronica and we were part of the congregation. It seems that they felt that not enough was being done to find her, as did the hostel matron, who returned to the police station every day looking for news, but receiving none.

It is now clear that even an immediate and vigorous search would probably not have saved Veronica, as she was almost certainly dead before she was even reported missing – but that was not known at the time. It was an era when even the term 'serial killer' had barely been coined, and it would be some time before that possibility was even entertained. Had the truth about her disappearance, however, been discovered earlier than sixteen months after her death, it has to be said that the terrible possibility remains that the lives of some or all of the other girls might have been saved. Ten days elapsed before the murder of Tania, and another nineteen days before Julie's death. It would be seven weeks from Veronica's death before the killing stopped. There was time to stop the terrible sequence of events for the girls after Veronica. It was not until the second body was discovered accidentally in April 1979 that work began on missing person files and a pattern emerged, thanks to the work of Sergeant Bob Giles (who has never received any recognition from the government for his important work in this case). Concern about frightening the public held the police back from making these issues public until in January 1979, when the Mykyta family agreed to speak to the media.

This and the ensuing publicity, combined with a substantial reward being offered, drew out an informant who led the police to Amelia and ultimately led to Miller's arrest. The police search of the Truro area after the second body was found resulted in the finding of the third and fourth bodies on the opposite side of the road. It is still a mystery how those remains were not found earlier when they were only a hundred metres from Veronica's resting place, as all the bodies in Swamp Road were not buried, just roughly covered with branches.

In hindsight, it seems to me that the initial response was somewhat inadequate, and greatly influenced by an assumption that these were runaway, badly behaved girls. We know that this impression was still held until after the conclusion of the trial and was strengthened by the media. In defence, however, of the police force, I think that there were several mitigating factors:

1. It was Christmas Eve when Veronica was reported missing. The matron of the hostel was not deterred by her heavy workload and busy Christmas events and reported to the police station on 24 and 25 December, and every day thereafter, according to her recollection now. Nevertheless, the police station would have been trying to close down, maybe to a skeleton staff, for the Christmas break. Even if they had wanted to interview the hotel and shop staff, the Christmas public holidays would have made that more difficult than normal.

In addition, in 1976, Christmas Day and Boxing Day were on Saturday and Sunday, so the following Monday and Tuesday, 27th and 28th, would have been taken as public holidays, resulting in a four-day break, with all the shops closed. That whole week through to the New Year would have been a holiday period. It is probable, however, that the Majestic Hotel, in front of which Veronica was taken, would have been open and very busy.

2. In the days before computerisation and databases, information was manually recorded and stored, and we know that missing person reports were typically filed on library-style cards and filed in boxes. We are told that around that time there would have been at least 3,000 of these cards created annually, and that there was no way other than manual handling to draw out information about these cases as we can today with sorting a data base. When the police finally examined their records for patterns of disappearance, that was what had to happen – hours and hours of reading and memory-based cross-referencing. Senior and retired police who remember this case and others all admit that it would have been very different today.

3. The bodies were not found for a long time after the event, and were not found at the same time. Almost exactly a year passed between the mushroom hunters finding Veronica's remains and the bush walkers finding Sylvia's body. There was no forensic evidence and dental charts had to be utilised for identification (even that technology was very new). It was even proposed that Veronica had wandered into the bush, become lost and died of thirst – a highly improbable scenario, but suggested for lack of any other explanations. Instead of alarm bells, there was simply a long silence.

Once, however, the police realised that they were dealing with a serial killer, they swung into action. As recounted by Ken Thorsen when I spoke to him in Adelaide in 2017, the police were recovering from 'the fiasco of the Beaumont investigation', in which three children were abducted from the beach and were never found. Serious blunders marred the handling of the case and when Thorsen realised that they had serial killings on their hands he was determined to do the job properly. Allowing for the constraints of the pre-computer era and the lack of forensic evidence, they did succeed in finding the remaining perpetrator quickly and were successful in obtaining a conviction and long sentence. That outcome is in stark contrast to the case of the Beaumont children. They have never been found in over fifty years, although fresh leads have emerged and been dismissed even as I write.

Thorsen explained that after Commissioner Draper returned from a trip to the UK, he was charged with forming a new Major Crimes Investigation Unit; if he, ranked as an inspector at the time, declared a major crime to have taken place, he was empowered to bring in enough manpower to do the legwork required to expedite an outcome. This was unlike the Beaumont investigation, where, in his opinion, there were 'too many chiefs and not enough Indians'. Thus when Veronica's body was found, Thorsen was already in place with his new unit.

When Sergeant Bob Giles later discovered the pattern of missing girls, he actually brought nine records to show to Thorsen, who put the information in front of the deputy commissioner when he returned from holidays. The story played out from there as already told in this account (seven of them were relevant). Inspector Thorsen was able to call on as many police officers as he required, including police cadets, mounted police and the dog squad, to carry out the biggest search in South Australian police history.

Therefore, from where I stand, it seems that the police response was minimal at the time of Veronica's disappearance, as a result of some inadequacies due to lack of urgency as well as lack of resources and tools, and, in addition, some factors beyond their control. By the time the body was found in 1979, however, a full and robust police response ensured that the remaining perpetrator was apprehended relatively quickly.

Most importantly, the decision of the police to take James Miller out to the burial places on the night of his arrest made sure that the families were able to reclaim the remains of their children and find some closure to the tragic events. I am sure that each of the families is grateful for that decision. As a member of Veronica's wider circle of friends and people who cared for her, I am also grateful for the good work done by the police to conclude this case, even if there is no conviction on record for the killing of Veronica.

Other questions

Many other questions will probably never be answered. Some of them concern Miller's stories – his police interview, his unsworn statement from the dock and his account written in prison – all of which have inconsistencies. Clearly, they cannot all be true, but I suspect the time is long past for any more truth to emerge. I have raised some of these questions as part of the narrative; in particular, the issue of where the victims were actually killed and what part Miller played in the tragic saga.

The other important question that arises from Miller's stories is the issue of what happened to all the other girls that he says he and Worrell picked up in the car and then let out safely. If, as he asserted, there were at least dozens of these girls (this was part of his argument to establish that he could not have possibly known which ones Worrell would kill), where were they when the news of the murders broke? Why did they not emerge with stories of lucky survival, thankful that they had not become victims? In 1981, *The News* ran a story about a woman who purported to have survived an attack by Worrell in 1974; she was sworn to silence in exchange for her life, but this seems to be the only record of someone who escaped.[55] The two perpetrators were very distinctive – one older, one younger and supposedly handsome with distinctive long hair. It is unbelievable that any of these girls would not remember their ride with them and be shocked when they realised how close they came to tragic ends. If these girls did not exist, and it is highly likely that they don't, it lends weight to the argument that the predators targeted the seven victims, that the only girls they picked up were killed, and that Miller therefore knew exactly what was going to happen.

Another question remains about the reward proffered by the government and the newspaper. The reward was paid out in the end, but not to Amelia, as is claimed on many of the popular sites and accounts – Thorsen confirmed that fact to me in our interview. It remains confidential but there is some reference to a member of the public who named Amelia to the police, and others who say that it was someone who was in prison. Although some people will know for certain, that detail will probably remain a secret. It does not impinge on my story of Veronica but was the critical action that cracked the case and led the police directly to Miller.

It leads me to another question about human behaviour. It is beyond comprehension now to those of us who know the story, that Amelia failed to report the conversation she had with Miller to the police for over two years. As it occurred after Worrell's death by car accident, it would not have saved the victims, nor prevented any others, but it would have led the police immediately to Miller and saved the grief-stricken families two years of desperate waiting and agony. In addition, Miller would have been incarcerated earlier, as he richly deserved. Amelia's version is that she thought it did not matter, as Worrell was dead, she was not sure of the truth of the story, and that she had compassion on Worrell's mother. I cannot judge Amelia's conscience but find her decision difficult to understand. It was compounded by her unclear and self-contradictory testimony in court.

My last questions fittingly concern Veronica herself. Forty years after the event, I have researched all that I could possibly find about her life and her last days and movements. Needless to say, there is still conjecture in the way I have told her story. As recounted in the narrative, I was surprised to find people who were involved with her and the case still alive with strong memories when I travelled to Adelaide in 2017. Someone I have not been able to find is her friend who accompanied her into the city on that fateful night. Is Jenny still alive? If she was about the same age as Veronica, she would be about sixty now, and could well be still alive. I would love to ask her about that last night.

Why did they separate? Did Veronica tell her to go on ahead or did Jenny see the bus approaching and just decide to go without her? How did she feel over those early days after the disappearance? Where was she when Veronica's body was recovered? How has the rest of life gone for her? The memories of that fateful last night must surely have stayed with her and been a burden of sadness over the years, perhaps mitigated by the memory of a happy friendship.

Most of all, I still have unanswered questions about Veronica's family. Although she became a ward of the state as a baby because her mother died, her father was still alive. She possibly had siblings, who could still be alive now, and half-siblings if her father remarried. In addition, there would certainly be an extended family of aunts, uncles and cousins. I never met them and failed in my quest to discover any personal information about them because of the strict privacy laws in state institutions. Nor can I ascertain exactly where she lived as a young child. Were there any other foster homes and families? Who are the families she was sitting with, and with whom she is evidently celebrating Christmas together in the photos from her album? So the questions remain, and I ask for the forgiveness of any family members for writing this book without their permission. I hope that they will accept this story as a gift to Veronica, whom we loved like a daughter. Perhaps these or others will help fill out the missing parts so that Veronica's story can be told more completely.

All these questions and many others will just have to be held lovingly in tension as we wait to meet Veronica in eternity. And then they won't be important any more.

References

Chapter 4
1. Miller & Wordley, 1984, p. 21
2. Cornwall, 2002, p. 92
3. Ibid., p. 94
4. Wilson & Simmonds, 2000, p. 71
5. Miller & Wordley, 1984

Chapter 5
6. Ibid., p. 45

Chapter 6
7. Bricknell & Renshaw, 2016, p. 1
8. Swanton et al., 1988. p. 113
9. Ibid., p. 116
10. De Ionno & Whittington, 1979
11. Swanton et al., 1988, p. 33
12. Mykyta, 1981, p. 7

Chapter 7
13. Miller & Wordley, 1984, p. 90

Chapter 8
14. Burnett, 1978

Chapter 10
15. Mykyta, 1981, pp. 64–65
16. Ibid., p. 66
17. de Luca, 1979
18. Hunt, 2008
19. Wilson & Simmons, 2000, p. 75
20. Hunt, 2008
21. Ibid.
22. Mykyta, p. 75
23. Ibid., p. 82
24. DeIonno & Whittington, 1979

Chapter 11
25. Brown, 1993

Chapter 12
26. Miller & Wordley, 1984, p. 100
27. *The Western Australian*, 1979
28. Ibid., pp. 101–102
29. Wilson & Simmonds, 2000, p. 78
30. Miller & Wordley, 1984, p. 126
31. De Ionno, 1979
32. Mykyta, 1981, p. 106

Chapter 13
33. Australian Government, 2004
34. Ibid.
35. Ibid.
36. Ibid.
37 Australian Government, 2014

Chapter 14
38. De Ionno, 1980
39. Australian Law Reform Commission, 1986
40. De Ionno, 1980
41. Hunt, 2013
42. De Ionno, 1980

Chapter 15
43. Mykyta, 1982, p. 197
44. Swanton et al., 1980, p. 34

Chapter 21
45. Cornwall, 2002, p. 91
46. Ibid., p. 97
47. Ibid., p. 175

Chapter 22
48. Wordley, 1979
49. Hunt, 2002

Chapter 24
50. Edwards, 2008

Appendix
51. Morgan, et al., 1984, p. 4
52. Ibid., p. 1
53. Cornwall, 2002, pp. 94–97
54. Miller & Wordley, 1984, p. 18
55. De Luca, 1981

Bibliography

Australian Broadcasting Commission. (2008). *Truro Killer Dies*. Retrieved from: http://www.abc.net.au

Australian Government. (2004). *Forgotten Australians: A Report on Australians who Experienced Institutional or Out-Of-Home care as Children*. Retrieved from: http://www.forgottenaustralians.com

— (2014). *Find and Connect*. Retrieved from: https://www.findandconnect.gov.au

Australian Law Reform Commission.(1986). *General Issues of Evidence and Procedure: Unsworn Statements. Recognition of Aboriginal Customary Laws*. Retrieved from: www.alrc.gov.au

Bricknell, S. & Renshaw, L. (2016). Missing persons in Australia 2008–2015. *Statistical Bulletin 1* Retrieved from https://aic.gov.au

Brown, K. (1993). The Truro Murders in retrospect: a historical review of the identification of the victims. *Annals Academy of Medicine Singapore*. 22(1):103–6. Retrieved from: https://www.ncbi.nih.gov

Burnett, R. (27 May 1978). Police fear woman killed. *The Advertiser*.

Cornwall, C. (2002). *The Punishment Fit the Crime: memoirs of a probation and parole officer*. Adelaide, Australia: Peacock Publications.

De Ionno, P. (25 May 1979). Mummified body was curled up like a cat. *The Advertiser*.

— (21 February 1980). Truro court told girls took lifts with men. *The Advertiser*.

— (11 March 1980). Just chauffeur and the mug: Miller. *The Advertiser*.

— (March 13 1980). Jury out for eight hours. Miller guilty of six Truro murders. *The Advertiser*.

De Ionno, P. & Whitington B. (12 May 1979). 'Truro'. *The Advertiser*.

De Luca, G. (24 January 1979). 'Is Julie a murder victim?', *The News*.

— (15 April 1981). 'I Survived'. *The News*.

Dowseley, F. (2003). A review of the needs of co-victims of homicide. *Current Issues in Criminal Justice*. 26; 15(2) pp. 186–192. Retrieved from: http://www.austlii.edu.au

Edwards, V. (2008, 24 October). Pain eased for some by Truro killer's death. *The Australian*. Retrieved from: https://www.theaustralian.com.au

Green, E. (1993). *The Intent to Kill: Making Sense of Murder*. Baltimore, USA: Clevedon Books.

Green, R. (2017). *The Truro Murders: The sex killing spree through the eyes of an accomplice*. (n.p.) Green.

Hunt, N. (23 November 2002). 'The model parolee who was really a killer'. *The Advertiser*.

— (26 October 2008). 'Another Truro "now unlikely"'. *The Sunday Mail*. Retrieved from: https://www.adelaidenow.com.au

— (23 April 2013). 'The hunt for the Truro serial killers Christopher Worrell and James Miller was the biggest police probe in South Australian history'. *The Sunday Mail*.

Kidd, Paul B. *The Truro Serial Murders: The Horrifying Discoveries*. TruTV.com (n.d.).

Miller, J.W., & Wordley, D. (1984). *Don't Call Me Killer*. Melbourne, Australia: Harbourtop Productions.

Mykyta, A. (1981). *It's a long way to Truro*. Melbourne, Australia: McPhee Gribble.

The Western Australian. (27 April 1979) p1.(n.a.).

Wilson, P., & Simmonds, J.W. (2000). *Murder in Tandem: When 2 People Kill*. Sydney, Australia: Harper Collins.

Wordley, D. (3 June 1979). 'Parole Chief fires back at the critics'. *The Sunday Mail*.

Thanks

Sketches by Viktor Bohdan, courtroom artist, used by permission.

Map of bush area near Truro from Google maps.

Photographs of Minda Home and McNally Training Centre from Find and Connect.

Photograph of the search at Truro from *The Sunday Mail*, 23 April 2013.

Cover portrait of Veronica © Peter Woods 2018.

Photograph of Charles Cornwall used by permission.

Photograph of mounted police officer Harry Brewer at Largs Bay used by permission.

Archive box of Anne-Marie Mykyta accessed with assistance from the State Library of South Australia.

Documents and cuttings made available by Ken Thorsen and Charles Cornwall.

www.ingramcontent.com/pod-product-compliance
Lightning Source LLC
Chambersburg PA
CBHW070859080526
44589CB00013B/1132